Readable & Maintai Code in Java

Dedicated to my wife Kamini Kumari

Author information

For any help please contact :
Amazon Author Page :
amazon.com/author/ajaykumar
Email : ajaycucek@gmail.com ,
 ajaxreso@gmail.com
Linkedin :
https://www.linkedin.com/in/ajaycucek
Facebook :
https://www.facebook.com/ajaycucek
Youtube :
 https://www.youtube.com/channel/UC1uXE
ebtqCLYxVdzirKZGIA
Twitter : https://twitter.com/ajaycucek
Instagram :
https://www.instagram.com/ajaycucek/
Skype : ajaycucek

Table of contents

Module 1 : Book Overview

Book Overview

Have you ever worked on a project that had terrible code? You need to develop it and maintain it, and on a daily basis, you wish that people before you did a better job. But are you absolutely sure that you write clean and maintainable code? If not, you should read this book. Some of the major topics that we will cover include the importance of naming and how to choose great names for your classes, variables, and methods; pitfalls of Java constructors, methods, tests, comments, and exception handling, and how you can either prevent or overcome them; as well as hands-on practical tips how you can maintain the top quality of your code. By the end of this book, you will gain the ability to do just that, write code that you and others will enjoy reading and working with. Before beginning the course, you should have some professional experience with Java in any

3

IDE, such as IntelliJ or Eclipse, and be able to write object-oriented code.

Module 2 : Clean and Maintainable Code Concepts

Introduction

There were times when the code was easy to understand, and there were also times when you would stare at code for longer periods of time trying to figure out what the code does. So various questions start to pop up in your head. Is it because I'm not experienced enough? Do I need another five years of experience to get to another level where I would really understand all code that I encounter? Or is it because the code I'm looking at is terrible? I'd like to make a guess and say that you have probably thought more than once that it is your problem, that the code is just fine, and it's you who needs more practice and more experience. I certainly have. While professional self-development is certainly a life-long process, I can assure you that dirty, unreadable code is widespread, and thousands of lines of bad code must have been written since you started reading this book. And there is one more kind of question that you might be asking yourself. How do I know if I write good professional code? How do I make sure that the code that I produce is not going to trigger a what the heck is this reaction from people who will read my code. And in this book, I will make an attempt to answer this question. As Donald Knuth says, "The best programs are written so that computing machines can perform them quickly and so that human beings can understand them clearly. " So in this book, we're going to discuss how to write Java code that is easy for other human beings to read, maintain, and understand.

Benefits of Clean Code

I'm sure that you already realize that clean code is something good and everyone should strive for, but I'd like to discuss for a moment that clean code is not a nice to have. It's practically a necessity. First of all, sloppy code leads to a decrease in understanding, which in turn leads to bugs. Are bugs bad? Just ask the UK traffic control when they had to deal with chaos on a cold December day because of a software bug or the senior management of a finance institution, Knight Capital Group, that lost almost half a billion dollars in 30 minutes. So yes, bugs are bad. But sloppy code doesn't just mean a bug that becomes someone else's problem. Bad code is technical debt, and technical debt means slower and slower development. This means that in a new project, you might spend 50% of your time coding and 50% reading code. With time, and that is the case for most people, you spend over 90% of your time just reading code. To quote Robert Martin,

"Indeed the ratio of time spent reading versus writing is well over 10 to 1. We are constantly reading old code as part of the effort to write new code therefore making it easy to read makes it easier to write. " What this means is that if you want to spend time writing code and build cool new features, you need to spend less time reading it, so you need to write clean code in the first place. So please don't treat bad code and technical debt like some abstract concept that doesn't affect you. It's just as real as credit card debt. The longer you ignore it, the worse it is down the road. That's how I see technical debt, and I suggest you do the same. It's okay to have it sometimes, but you want to get rid of it as fast as possible. So if everything I have said wasn't enough to convince you that clean code is important, let me say that above all, clean code benefits you. Sooner or later, you will have to deal with your own code from six months ago or maybe a year ago. If you wrote clean code back then, you will definitely be grateful to yourself.

Who Is this book for?

So who is this book for? Developers, obviously. They have to deal with it so they naturally care about it. If the team doesn't, job satisfaction gradually decreases until it hits rock bottom. Test automation engineers. They should not only care about code quality, they should absolutely promote it at every occasion because they are quality assurance professionals. Test automation engineers write automated tests based on the requirements and also the testing framework to support it. A testing framework may need to know how to do a lot of things, UI testing, communication over HTTP, making database queries, and much more. So code quality is just as important for automation professionals. Ironically, I have seen rather large in-house test automation frameworks in a very poor state, which means that some QA professionals are so focused on testing other people's work that they don't control the quality of their own work. So anyone who writes automated tests should absolutely care about code quality. Project managers should care as well. I'm not saying project managers need to participate in code refactoring, but they must understand the importance of technical debt and allocate time and budget for it if the team says they need to remove it. However, to avoid confusion, I should highlight that this isn't a book for project managers. This book is all about coding, so the focus groups are developers and test automation engineers.

Prerequisites

The main requirement for this book is that you know how to program in Java, you know the syntax, and you are comfortable writing simple object-oriented programs. I'd say this is the minimum for you to benefit from this book. If you have at least six months of professional experience in a Java software project, that's even better. Other than that, there is no need to know any special framework or tool. I do expect that you have the JDK installed on your computer and you use some kind of code editor. When we start, I will already have Java installed, and I will use IntelliJ as my IDE. But if you're using Eclipse, NetBeans, or something else, that's also fine.

Book Overview

- **Naming Matters**
- **Better Constructors**
- **Implementing Methods**
- **Handling Exceptions**
- **Class Organization**
- **Writing Comments**
- **Improving Tests**
- **Maintaining Clean Code**

Let's briefly take a look at all the things we're going to cover step by step. We'll start off with the topic how to name things, how to best name classes, methods, and variables. If it seems like a trivial matter to you, then it is almost certain that you have room for improvement in this area. Naming is so crucial that it's arguably the most important topic of this book. We'll then move on and talk about constructors. Obviously, there is no need to discuss how to name constructors. It's the same as your class. But in certain situations, constructors can get pretty messy as well, so we need to talk about them. Next, methods and everything that goes on inside of them. This is the meatiest module, and it contains a lot of useful information. Most things that can go wrong are usually related to methods. After that, we'll look at exception handling. Strictly speaking, exception handling happens inside methods, but the topic is pretty big, so I decided to split it out into a separate module. Then classes. We'll discuss the what and the how, what a class should contain, and how it should be organized. After that, comments. It might seem redundant to make an entire module about comments, but I will do my best to show you that this is not the case. Comments can be abused in so many ways that it truly deserves a separate discussion. We'll then move on to testing. Automated tests aren't production code, but they are code nonetheless, and they are governed by slightly different rules and best practices, so it's worth talking about it. Finally, we'll explore the ways how you can maintain clean code. Clean code is never a goal that is achieved once. It's a continuous process, practically a daily effort. So if producing clean code is climbing a mountain, then this module will show you how to stay on top of that mountain.

Always Code as if...

Before we begin, allow me to sneak in another quote. It's a quote that made the biggest impact on me. It really made me want to improve my own code, and I sincerely hope it makes a similar impression on you. It reads as follows, "Always code as if the guy who ends up maintaining your code will be a violent psychopath who knows where you live. " I think that is brilliant. It's funny, yet very convincing and is spot on.

With this in mind, let's see how we can write code that wouldn't make other people too nervous.

Module 3 : Naming Matters

Introduction

In this module of this book, we are going to discuss naming. If someone asked me to talk about one topic on clean code, I think I would choose to talk about naming. I truly believe it's one of the most important aspects of coding, yet somehow, it is also one thing that people tend to underestimate. Ironically, the concept of naming is the easiest to understand, but sometimes difficult to get right. As I already mentioned in the previous module, we spend most of our time reading code. Sometimes up to 90% of our time is reading, so it shouldn't be a struggle. You shouldn't look at code and spend valuable time thinking, what's the purpose of this class, or what kind of data this field contains, or what this method really does. The ideal situation is when you can glance through the code and get the gist of it right away. So in this module, we are going to talk about naming best practices.

- Class Names
- Variable Names
- Method Names

- Common Guidelines

We'll discuss how to name classes and what naming patterns we should avoid. We'll then move on to variables and methods, each has specific rules, best practices, and pitfalls. We will then sum up with common naming tips that apply to all of the above.

Classes: Best Practices

Noun
- Concrete: Dog, House, Calculator
- Abstract: SalaryAlgo, EmailSender
Specific

Let's start with the basics. A class name should be a noun. When you create an object, an instance of a class, it should be a thing. It can be something that physically exists, a dog, a cat, a house, a table, or a calculator. It can also be an abstract thing, for example, a SalaryAlgo or an EmailSender. Whatever it is, try and make it a noun. Another important aspect is that it should be specific. How specific? There is almost never a clear-cut answer, but let me try and compare a Java class with a labeled box, and the box is labeled Stuff. Stuff is a noun, so that's good. But what do you think is in there? It could be anything, right? If you have one such box, that's not a big deal perhaps. But if you have many boxes with vague names and you're searching for your house keys, then that will take you a while. So what kind of a real problem do you get with classes with nonspecific names? They become huge. They become a place where people dump code if they don't know where to put it or can't be bothered. So this breaks the SRP, the Single Responsibility Principle. A class should have a single responsibility, or more precisely, one reason to change. Now let's move on to some examples of classes with bad names and see if we can do anything about them.

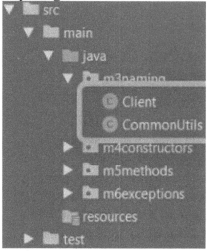

Let's say we have two classes, CommonUtils and Client. I suppose CommonUtils is a more obvious example because it contains the word Common, which isn't specific at all. It probably has a whole bunch of unrelated things, just like a box labeled Stuff. So we'll have to look inside the class to figure out what it does. On the other hand, we have the class Client, and it seems to be fine. Client is a noun, and it's short and simple, but is it specific? What kind of a client? As in a human customer of a business? I'm not so sure, so we'll have to take a look inside as well. So let's do that. First, the Utils class.

```
package m3naming;
import java.time.Instant;
import java.time.ZoneId;
import java.util.Random;
```

```java
public class CommonUtils {
    public static int
countOccurrences(String stringToSearch,
char charToFind) {
        int count = 0;
        for (int i = 0; i <
stringToSearch.length(); i++) {
            if (stringToSearch.charAt(i)
== charToFind) {
                count++;
            }
        }
        return count;
    }
    public static void
printNowNewYorkTime() {
        String now =
Instant.now().atZone(ZoneId.of("America/N
ew_York")).toString();
        System.out.println(now);
    }
    public static int
generateRandomNumberBetween(int low,
int high) {
        return new Random().nextInt(high
- low) + low;
    }
    public static double convertCurrency() {
        return 0;
    }
}
```

If we inspect the methods that it contains,
we'll find that it contains generic helper
methods that aren't related to any specific
business logic. There is one that searches and
counts a specific character inside a string,
there is one that prints the current time in
New York, and yet another one that
generates random numbers within a specific

range. All of these methods might be useful, but they are all unrelated. One deals with strings, the other with time, and the last one with numbers. So if we had to rename our class as is, we would need to call it StringAndTimeAndNumberUtils, which is rather ugly. The solution here is to simply split the class into smaller classes.

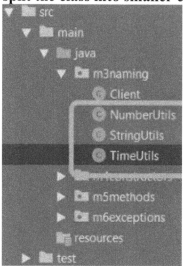

There, we now have several classes, one called StringUtils, the other TimeUtils, and the last one NumberUtils. Yes, this resulted in several tiny classes, each with a single method, so this seems like an overkill, but it's very likely that you will fill these up with more methods over time. Moving on.

```
package m3naming;
import org.apache.http.HttpResponse;
import java.io.IOException;
public class ClientDemo {
    public static void main(String[] args)
throws IOException {
        HttpResponse response = new
WebHttpClient().sendGet("https://api.githu
b.com/");
```

```
            }
}
```

Now let's take a look at the client, and we'll first look at what it does inside the main method. As you can see, we create a new Client object and then invoke the method send, which means our client can send something, we don't know what exactly, and it sends something to a URL and receives a response. This doesn't seem to fit our previous guess. It doesn't look like it's a business client.

```
package m3naming;
import org.apache.http.HttpResponse;
import org.apache.http.client.HttpClient;
import
org.apache.http.client.methods.HttpGet;
import
org.apache.http.impl.client.CloseableHttpCli
ent;
import
org.apache.http.impl.client.HttpClientBuilde
r;
import java.io.IOException;
/**
 * An Http client
 */
public class Client {
   private HttpClient client =
getDefaultClient();
   public HttpResponse sendGet(String s)
throws IOException {
      return client.execute(new HttpGet(s));
   }
   private CloseableHttpClient
getDefaultClient(){
      return HttpClientBuilder.create()
         .build();
   }
```

}

And if we look inside the class, we can even see that there is some Java docs saying that this is a client for sending HTTP requests. Ah, so this class isn't even about a human client. It's a program client that knows how to talk to a web service, but we had to go and look inside the class to find that out. And if it weren't for the Java doc, we'd need to further scan the class, for example, looking inside this method, to see that it sends an HttpGet request. As you can see, the client seems to be specific, but was still confusing.So rename this class as WebHttpClient.java. So in this chapter, we ended up fixing classes with bad names, and we used two techniques, one is split, and the other one is rename. Simple, but makes your code a lot clearer.

Classes: Prefer Concrete Names

Avoid :
- *Coordinator
- *Manager
    - - e.g. StoreManager, FlightManager

You will often encounter a situation when your class is responsible for delegating tasks to other classes. Something like a coordinator class that just brings other classes together. In this case, people often add a suffix coordinator or manager, RespositoryManager, StoreManager, FlightManager, and so forth. The problem with this name is that it's still too vague.

Managing often means a whole range of tasks. It's okay to name an entire application a manager(like "Flight Reservation Manager"), but a single class, probably not. You might as well stick half of your application code into that manager class. Some Alternatives :

- Builder
- Writer
- Reader
- Handler
- Container

There is no hard rule how to name such classes, but I would at least like to suggest some of the below alternatives with narrower scope such as builder, writer, reader, handler, or container. You may be familiar with the concept of patterns. For example, you have creational patterns such as the Builder, Singleton, or Factory. But how is this related to the topic of clean code and naming classes? The thing is, you might encounter classes whose names contain these patterns. You might see a CarFactory class, and that is supposed to tell you that this class is responsible for creating car objects. There is also an HttpClientBuilder class in this Apache library, and that one also builds and return an object, but using the Builder pattern, which uses method chaining. And that's fine. That's valid. This is a widespread practice, and I personally see no harm in it, but please don't overdo it. As you learn more patterns and generally become more advanced, please don't clutter the names with fancy terms. CarFactory? How about a SingletonCarFactory or an AbstractSingletonCarFactory? If we add

ProxyHandler from the other side, does it make it any better? I don't think so, and I promise I'm not exaggerating.

A Real Class from Spring Framework : J2eeBasedPreAuthenticatedWebAuthenticationDetailsSource

For example, this class actually exists and is part of the popular Java Spring Framework. I even had to reduce the font size to fit it on the slide. Even if there was a good reason for such a name, I wouldn't want to be the maintainer of that code base. So please, try and keep your class names short, specific, and simple to the best of your ability.

Variables

Variable Name Guidelines :
- Never a single letter
- Always specific
- Ideally 1-2 words
- booleans prefixed with "is", for example isActive or isValid
- use camelCase
- use ALL_CAPS with underscores for constants

Good variable names are easier to come up with than class names; however, they are just as important. Here are some basic guidelines. Never a single letter or an obscure abbreviation; always specific; ideally, one/two words, Booleans should be prefixed with is, for example, isActive or isValid; use camelCase; and use all caps with underscores for constants. The last two aren't actually guidelines, but generally accepted conventions.

```
Map<String, String> d = getThings()
```

So let's use an incremental example. Yes, the method name is vague and bad, but I did that on purpose so we can concentrate on the variable. So you ask the author of this code, what is d? He says that d stands for data, and here is our first rule, never name your variables with a single letter. So you modify this to data. Great!

```
Map<String, String> data = getThings();
```

But what kind of data? Is it tomorrow's weather forecast or some secret FBI files? After some investigation, you find that the method returns personal details about a customer.

```
Map<String, String> customerDetails = getThings();
```

So now we can rename this to customerDetails, and now we can say that this is a specific name in camelCase and fits within the recommended limit of two words. Based on what we have seen, we can make an improvement to our code(ClientDemo.java). Instead of a single letter r, we should rename this to a full single word, response. We could name it HttpResponse, but we already have the type here that says exactly the same thing, so response is enough. Alright, let's move on to methods.

Methods: Best Practices

One can potentially spend half an hour discussing how to best name methods, but I will limit everything to just two points.

Methods should reveal intent, and you should understand precisely what the method does just by looking at the name, not how it does it, but what. This leads us to one single rule. If you have to look inside the method to understand what it does, you can probably improve the name. That's it. No more, no less.

Verb (Do What?)		Noun (To What?)		Result
load	+	Page	=	loadPage()
set	+	Price	=	setPrice()
convert	+	Currency	=	convertCurrency()

To achieve this, try and use the template that you see above. Methods are actions, but we also need to say what the action applies to. So not just load. Load what? Load a page. Not just set, but set something specific, like a new price and so on. If you follow this template, you should be fine most of the times. If you remember the rule about being specific, then that's even better.

Verb (Do What?)		Noun (To What?)		Result
load	+	~~Data~~ customerDetails	=	loadCustomerDetails()
set	+	~~Value~~ Price	=	setPrice()

Not loadData, but loadCustomerData. Not setValue, but setPrice. Specific is good. Vague is bad.

Map<String, String> customerDetails = getThings();

Previously, we saw an example with a method called getThings. We already figured out that we are talking about customer data, so now we can also rename the method to something specific, like getCustomerData.

```
Map<String, String> customerData =
getCustomerData();
```
In our code example(ClientDemo.java), we
had a method called send. And if we apply
the rules that we talked about, we could
rename it to sendRequest. Actually, that isn't
great either. It's better. We now know that
this method doesn't send an email, for
example, but what kind of a request? Again,
we have to look inside the method to see that
it sends a get request. So we can either
rename to sendGetRequest or just sendGet.
Both are valid options. One is more explicit
and verbose. The other is shorter. I'd go for
the shorter version because the class name
HttpClient provides enough context that tells
these are going to be HTTP requests.
```
"aa".concat("b").endsWith("b")
```
Finally, I'd like to highlight that everything
I've said aren't hard rules. If they were,
things would be easy. Sometimes it's
perfectly fine to have single-word methods.
Here is a native Java example that
manipulates strings. These are string
methods present on the string class. The first
method is a single word, not two words, and
the second method doesn't have a noun, and
despite that, the code is perfectly readable.

Methods: Antipatterns

Alright, we talked about what to do when it
comes to method naming. Let's now talk
about the opposite. By that, I mean what
patterns you should avoid.
Method Name Anti-patterns :

- Method does more than the name says
- Name contains "and", "or", "if"

First, make sure your methods really do what they say they do. If your method name says ConvertCurrency, but it also changes the state of another object or the value of a global variable, then that's a side effect, and you should remove it. This leads us to the second point. If you end up saying this method does A and B, that is a clear indicator that the method does multiple things and should be split. The same goes for words like or and if.

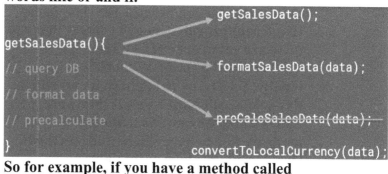

So for example, if you have a method called getSalesData and inside you see that it queries a database for data, formats that data in some way, and then also runs some algorithms, like precalculations, then the method name lies. Of course, you don't change it to getAndFormatAndPrecalculateSalesData. Instead, you split the code into three smaller methods, getSalesData, formatSalesData, and preCalcSalesData. The last method name is actually a bit vague. It's unclear what kind of precalculations we're doing, so that breaks my own suggestion from previous chapters. It should be a specific calculation, so perhaps, round up to dollar, or convert to local currency, or something like that.

Methods: Exceptions to the Rule

What we have covered so far applies to most cases But as it goes with every rule, there are exceptions, and I'd like to highlight some. Breaking Method Name Rules :

- **Static Factory Methods**
- **Builder and Fluent Interface patterns**

One is static factory methods, and I will talk about them in more detail in the next module about constructors. But for now, just know that frequently, they are not verbs, and the other typical exception happens with method chaining or a style called fluent interface. They focus on readability and try to make code look like human language.

someList.stream()
.map(func1.andThen(func2))
.findAny()
.orElseThrow(...);

For example, in Java 8, you have streams, and you get all sorts of methods, for example, orElseThrow or andThen. Additionally, such method chaining is used when creating a so-called domain-specific language. And you can apply that, for example, when creating automated tests.

Abbreviations and Spelling

Last but not least, I'd like to give you several simple tips that apply to classes, variables, and methods. First, don't use abbreviations. They are hard to read most of the time. Some abbreviations are okay, but you better make sure that they are completely universal such as kilos, kilometers, or pounds. But even with pounds, it's not obvious actually. Why? Because pounds aren't used worldwide. You have a lot of countries where grams and kilograms are used. So someone might look at your abbreviation and think uh, labs? What are labs? You can't know everyone's cultural background, so it's best to avoid abbreviations in 99% of cases. Also, keep an eye on bad spelling and fix it whenever possible. It's fast, easy, and brings some benefit, and I'm not saying that because I'm grammar obsessed. It's because it affects searching. let me give you an example. Imagine you have a very large project open in your IDE, perhaps a million lines of code. You need to implement a feature, and as part of that, you need to convert currency, and you're fairly sure you've seen such a method somewhere in the code base. So you open up Global Search and type convert. That doesn't produce any results. So you try currency, and that also doesn't help. And the reason is because the method does exist, but has two typos in it. Its name is covertCurency with a single R. If you search for long enough, you will probably find it, but imagine having to do this kind of guesswork five times a day every day. So I hope I've convinced you that spelling matters and has real negative impact on your day-to-day tasks.

Summary

Classes – Single Responsibility
Variables – descriptive and concise
Methods – reveal intent and no multi-tasking
Let's do a quick recap. We have discussed
the importance of correct naming. We have
talked about the convention that a class
name should be a noun and that classes
should have a single responsibility. And the
foundation of this principle is a name as
specific as possible. We then moved on to
variable names. Variable names should
ideally be one or two words and describe as
precisely as possible what it contains.
Finally, method names should be intent
revealing verbs or verbs with nouns; have no
side effects; and avoid and, or, if words. If
they do, such methods should be split into
smaller functions.

Module 4 : Better Constructors

Introduction

In this module, we are going to talk about
constructors. When you have simple objects
without many parameters, there isn't much
to talk about. But often, objects that we need
to create can be quite complex, and that

complexity can be further multiplied by business logic and rules. So things can go wrong when defining and using them.

Static Factory Methods
Constructor Chaining
Builder Pattern

So in this module, we are going to first look at the concept of static factory methods and how they benefit client code that needs to initialize an object. This is a scenario where you typically have a single constructor. We'll then look at a different scenario where we'll have several constructors and look at how chaining helps us write less boilerplate code and keep things dry. But that doesn't always help. You still might end up with what is called the constructor telescoping antipattern, and we'll see how the builder pattern helps us overcome this.

Static Factory Methods

How do you normally create an instance of some class? You use the new keyword.

new GregorianCalendar(new TimeZone() ,
new Locale ( ))

The thing is, even if you have just a single constructor, it can be fairly complex to create, for example, one that requires multiple arguments, and it doesn't look too bad until you realize just how much the TimeZone object requires to be created properly. You just wanted to do an operation with time, and you suddenly have to deal with all of this. So when you have extra logic how to create an object, code can become difficult. And I might hear you say, well, just wrap it into a common method, and yes, that's what I'm getting at. We can use a static factory method. In his book, Effective Java, Joshua Bloch suggests to consider static factory methods instead of constructors. You see static factory methods everywhere you look. As you can see, there are a lot of examples that are part of the Java language itself.

Static Factory Methods in Java :

- Calendar.getInstance();
- String.valueOf(true);
- LocalDate.of(2019, 01, 01);
- Optional.empty();
- Collections.unmodifiableCollection(...);

You might also think, hang on a second. These methods aren't following the suggested pattern of verb plus noun. GetInstance does, but empty, valueOf, and others aren't even verbs at all. And that's an accurate observation. But as I said in the previous module, some exceptions exist, and static factory methods are one of them. So what's the benefit of such methods? There are multiple, but the one we really want right now is that these methods can encapsulate all of the construction logic. You hide the verbosity and the complexity, so that becomes more readable. And if you want to change the creation of this object, you do so in a single class, not in 20 places, so that helps maintainability a lot. And indeed, compare the calendar creation with the static factory method. It's a single line. Of course, it's a single line because all of the construction is obstructed away from you as a user of this class. If we go inside, then we see that there is a lot of logic, but you don't need to care about it. You just call getInstance.

Constructor Chaining

```
package m4constructors;
public class BankAccount {
    private double balance;
    private double interest;
    BankAccount(){}
    BankAccount(double balance){
        if(balance < 0){
            throw new
IllegalArgumentException("Starting balance
can't be less than 0");
        }
        this.balance = balance;
    }
    BankAccount(double balance, double
interest){
        if(interest < 0){
            throw new
IllegalArgumentException("Interest rate
can't be less than 0");
        }
        if(balance < 0){
            throw new
IllegalArgumentException("Starting balance
can't be less than 0");
        }
        this.balance = balance;
        this.interest = interest;
    }
//getters and setters
}
```

Sometimes you decide to have several constructors. Let's say you have a class BankAccount, and you have one with the default null argument. This object needs to contain some useful information, so a starting balance would be nice, so you create a second constructor that takes a float or a double as a parameter. But some accounts have interest rate attached to them, so now you have another one that sets both the balance and the interest rate. Also, the requirements say that by default, all accounts should be created with a 1% interest rate. You notice that you already have some duplication. You set the fields multiple times, which means that this code isn't as DRY as it could be. Just a reminder, DRY means don't repeat yourself, which essentially means you should avoid code duplication. But this still doesn't look too bad, but then the requirements say that accounts may never be created with a negative balance or a negative interest rate. So you add a simple check to ensure that no one creates an account object with invalid arguments, but you have to keep the check in each constructor. Now this doesn't look as neat as before suddenly. And if the logic gets any more complicated, this would become a mess. In this situation, we can use chaining. I'll show you the end result. There, this looks a lot better.

```
package m4constructors;
class BankAccount2 {
    private double balance;
    private double interest;
    BankAccount2(){
        this(0);
    }
}
```

```
    BankAccount2(double balance){
        this(balance, 0.01);
    }
    BankAccount2(double balance, double
interest){
        if(interest < 0){
            throw new
IllegalArgumentException("Interest rate
can't be less than 0");
        }
        if(balance < 0){
            throw new
IllegalArgumentException("Starting balance
can't be less than 0");
        }
        this.balance = balance;
        this.interest = interest;
    }
//getters & setters
}
```

We have several constructors sorted in a
particular order from no arguments to one
argument to two arguments. Only the
bottom one has validation logic, so it's all in
one place, and it also sets the fields. So this
constructor does all of the heavy lifting. The
others just use this keyword and call it. This
could be further refactored. The interest rate
could be refactored into a constant since it is
a default value, and these argument checks
could be wrapped into prettier methods, but
that's a bit beyond the scope of this chapter
and module. The main takeaway is that you
should remember to use constructor
chaining to prevent duplication.

Constructor Telescoping

As their name suggests, constructors are meant to construct objects Sometimes objects are simple, and as such, you end up with simple ones that take one or two arguments, but things can get pretty complex as well.

```
Pizza(int size) { ... }
Pizza(int size, boolean cheese) { ... }
Pizza(int size, boolean cheese, boolean ham)
{ ... }
Pizza(int size, boolean cheese, boolean ham,
boolean mushroom) { ... }
```

Suppose you are building a backend system for a pizza restaurant, so you start off with a single parameter that takes the base size. But then it should also add cheese to all of your pizzas, but not necessarily all of them, so you create another one. And very soon, you end up with a long list, and the problem is multiplied by the simple fact that you should mix and match any number of ingredients. This is called the telescoping constructor pattern, and believe me, it's a mess. To overcome this challenge, you could use the builder pattern. The downside is that it involves some boilerplate code such as this inner Builder class; however, the end result is very readable code like this.

```
package m4constructors.pizzaexample;
class Pizza {
    static class Builder {
        //mandatory
        private final int size;
        // default is false
        private boolean cheese;
```

```java
        private boolean ham;
        Builder(int size) {
            this.size = size;
        }
        Builder cheese(boolean value) {
            cheese = value;
            return this;
        }
        Builder ham(boolean value) {
            ham = value;
            return this;
        }
        Pizza build() {
            return new Pizza(this);
        }
    }
    private Pizza(Builder builder) {
        int size = builder.size;
        boolean cheese = builder.cheese;
        boolean ham = builder.ham;
    }
}
package m4constructors.pizzaexample;
public class App {
    public static void main(String[] args){
        Pizza pizza = new Pizza.Builder(12)
                        .cheese(true)
                        .ham(true)
                        .build();
        // deliver pizza
    }
}
```

As you can see, multiple methods are chained together one after the other to build an object, and each method is responsible for setting one field. Obviously, this pattern can be applied to any situation where you need to build something with any random number of parameters. You could use it to build a game character, for example, or a car. I won't dive into more details about how exactly you should use this pattern as it is outside the scope of this book. The main purpose here is that you recognize this AntiPattern, and when you do, you should think, ah, this is getting pretty ugly. Perhaps I should apply the builder pattern.

Summary

- **Static Factory Methods**
- **Constructor chaining**
- **Builder and Fluent Interface**

Constructors are all about creating objects, and we have seen that creation is not always easy and straightforward. We have discussed that there is a danger of creating messy code if we don't anticipate an increase in complexity and just use the new keyword everywhere. instead, we can make use of static factory methods. If you have multiple constructors in your class, you should try and keep it as DRY as possible. This means you should minimize code duplication, and constructor chaining can help you out in some cases. Last, but not least, we have seen that certain programs require complex objects with many different parameter combinations, and in that case, applying the builder pattern is probably a good option.

Module 5 : Implementing Methods

Introduction

In this module, we are going to discuss everything, or almost everything, related to methods. In other languages, they are called functions, in Java, they are methods, and in the context of this book, it doesn't make a difference. One thing we are not going to talk about is naming methods because we covered that in the module about naming. So a method is where most of your programming happens. Classes are containers, and constructors are for creating objects, but the vast majority of application functionality is placed inside methods or functions, and is a consequence, most of dirty code revolves around them. So we'll approach methods in a structured way.

What methods should return
Parameters
Fail fast & return early
Avoid duplication
Conditionals

We'll first start at the surface and look at the method signature, what you should and should not return. Then we'll move on to parameters and what kind of best practices applies to them. After that, we'll take a look inside the methods. We'll talk about the fail-fast and return early principles and how they contribute to clean code, what kind of duplication we can encounter, and some simple techniques to avoid it. We'll then talk about conditionals and best ways to handle them.

Clean Code Concepts

Before we begin, I would like to go over several concepts. I thought about doing it in the very beginning of the book, but I believe that would result in too much theory in the beginning without practical examples, so I've decided to do it somewhere halfway through the book.

Clean Code Concepts :
- DRY vs. WET
- Cyclomatic Complexity
- Signal vs. Noise

So we have already seen DRY, which stands for don't repeat yourself. We apply DRY and remove duplication in constructor module by applying method chaining. And what's the opposite of DRY? You'd be surprised. It's WET, which stands for write everything twice or we enjoy typing. It's obviously just a sarcastic remark that should remind everyone to copy/paste as little as possible and instead refactor duplicate code into a single place. I wanted to mention this term because I might use it throughout this module and the rest of the book, and I wanted you to know about it. The next concept is cyclomatic complexity. This term might sound complicated, but the concept is fairly simple. Cyclomatic complexity is a software metric used to simply indicate the complexity of a program. How do you measure complexity? Well, discussing the formula is a bit outside the scope of this book, so I will just explain the essentials and the main point of this concept. Every time you use if, while, for, and, or, catch, and others, you are adding a bit of extra complexity. Some complexity is fine, but if you have too much of it in a single method, then that's bad. Why? Because complexity means a higher chance of mistakes, dirty code, and bugs. So in this module, we'll be talking about dirty code, and I'll be showing how to convert that to cleaner code. And often, you will find that the end result will have lower complexity as well. The last concept that I'd like to talk about is signal to noise ratio. Simply put, signal is code that is clear, expressive, and does one thing. If you see code that you easily understand, that's probably signal. Noise, on the other hand, is everything that prevents us from understanding code. Poor names is noise, high cyclomatic complexity is noise, duplication as well. Also, bad comments are a huge source of noise, so much that there is a separate module dedicated just to comments. I might hear you ask, did we already increase our signal to noise ratio in the previous modules when we improved variable names and refactored constructors? And the answer is yes. That's exactly what we achieved, and that's what we will continue doing throughout this book.

What (not) to Return

So let's start by looking at the method signature and see how returning something from a method can be a force for good and evil. As you know, methods can return either primitives, some kind of object, or null. And here is the first tip, avoid returning null as much as possible. Let's take a look at an example method that returns a list.

```
List<String> getSomeData() {
    try{ // read from DB }
    catch {
        // operation failed
        return null;
        return Collections.emptyList();
    }
}
```

That list might be populated from a database or from a file on disk. Obviously, this may fail for whatever reason. And if that happens, you might want to return null as if saying, sorry, I've got nothing for you. This means two things. You assume everyone will know about this internal implementation, and in my experience, it's much safer to assume that people don't know something. So if a caller doesn't know about null, they will hit a NullPointerException. Second, if the other person does know about that null, they have to add extra checks, if list is null. So what's wrong with this? First, the extra condition here adds cyclomatic complexity. It's not the end of the world, but nevertheless. Second, you have to write this check every time. Meaning, if you had to call this get method four or five times, then this extra if now has to be applied four or five times. Your code is gradually cluttered up by never-ending null checks, and that's noise. Instead, return an empty collection. This good practice is reflected by the fact that a static Collections.emptyList exists as part of a standard Java API. Return that instead of a null. This will mean that the client code can now be simplified to just one check, if list is empty. We have just reduced the amount of code to read and reduced cyclomatic complexity. So that covers null.

```
int withdraw(int amount) {
if (amount > balance) {
return -1;
}
else {
balance -= amount;
return 0;
}
}
```

There is one more thing that should be avoided most of the time, and that is returning special integers that act as error codes. Of course, it's completely fine to return an integer as some logical value, but it's not fine to return -1, 0, or something else if something bad happens. Why is this bad? Because -1 is a magic number with a magic meaning understandable only to you at the time of writing. If it doesn't make sense to others, then that's noise, not signal. And the second problem is that you will force client code to check for your magic number, which is a problem similar to null, but is actually even more obscure. If the operation returns a magic -1, then do something. And I have no idea what -1 means here. It might be -1 dollar, the final balance of the withdraw

operation. Instead, consider throwing an
exception.

```
void withdraw(int amount) throws
InsufficientFundsException {
if (amount > balance) {
throw new InsufficientFundsException();
}
balance -= amount;
}
```

In this case, it could be an illegal argument
exception explaining that there is not enough
money on the account or your own custom
exception.

Method Parameters

Enough with return types. Let's move on to
method arguments, and let's first of all talk
about how many arguments your method or
function should have. The general guideline,
and I would like to highlight the world
general, is fewer method arguments is better,
which sounds fairly simple, but it's not
always easy to follow. Let's zoom in on this
guideline. Try to have 0, 1, or 2 arguments.
Three arguments is not the end of the world,
but do try and avoid that. And if you have
four or more, you should consider
refactoring. Some typical examples of one-
argument methods are those that answer yes
or no questions, such as canReadFile and
you give it a file name. Another typical
example is a getter method that needs a
single input, for example,
getSalesDataForYear 2018 or something or
get getmedicalRecord for a specific person.
Typical two-argument methods can be

mathematical expressions such as adding, or multiplying, or asserting that two things are equal. You can find such assertEqual statements in both JUnit and TestNG testing frameworks. So what is the downside of having many arguments? Well, more arguments means more complexity, and we have already discussed that we want to keep cyclomatic complexity low. More arguments also means code that is difficult to read and understand.

Methods with 3+ Arguments Might:

- Do too many things (split it)
- Take too many primitive types (pass a single object)
- Takes a boolean(flag) argument (remove it)

If you find yourself writing a method with three, four, or more arguments, that it might suffer from any combination of the following. Your method does too many things, so you should split it into smaller methods. Alternatively, your methods might take too many primitive types instead of one single object. Also, it's possible that your method has unnecessary if-else logic based on a Boolean parameter, and we'll talk about Boolean flags in a separate chapter. Of course, this is not an exhaustive list, but these are very frequent causes. Let's take a look at several examples.

```
package m5methods;
import java.time.LocalDateTime;
import java.time.ZoneId;
import static java.time.LocalDateTime.now;
public class
MethodWithTooManyArguments {
    public static void main(String[] args){
```

```
    long millisSinceEpoch =
nowPlusTime(0, 0, 4);
    new
Order().setExpirationDate(millisSinceEpoch
);
  }
  private static long nowPlusTime(int
months, int weeks, int days) {
    return
LocalDateTime.now().plusMonths(months)
        .plusWeeks(weeks)
        .plusDays(days)
        .atZone(ZoneId.systemDefault())
        .toInstant()
        .toEpochMilli();
  }
}
```

In this example, we have an order, and you want to set the ExpirationDate that accepts a long primitive, and you can call the method nowPlusTime that requires three arguments, all of which are magic numbers. We'll talk about magic numbers separately. But right now, we have no idea what these numbers mean. Okay, let's look at the implementation. We can see that this method uses the Java 8 Time API, constructs a LocalDateTime object; adds months, weeks, and days; and then converts that to milliseconds. That's all fine, but what if we just need weeks or just days?

```
package m5methods;
import java.time.LocalDateTime;
import java.time.ZoneId;
import static java.time.LocalDateTime.now;
public class
MethodWithTooManyArguments {
  public static void main(String[] args){
```

```java
        new
Order().setExpirationDate(nowPlusDays(4));
    }
    public static long nowPlusMonths(int
months){
        checkTimeIsValid(months);
        return
toEpochMilli(now().plusMonths(months));
    }
    public static long nowPlusWeeks(int
weeks){
        checkTimeIsValid(weeks);
        return
toEpochMilli(now().plusWeeks(weeks));
    }
    public static long nowPlusDays(int days){
        checkTimeIsValid(days);
        return
toEpochMilli(now().plusDays(days));
    }
    private static long
toEpochMilli(LocalDateTime time){
        return
time.atZone(ZoneId.systemDefault())
            .toInstant()
            .toEpochMilli();
    }
    private static void checkTimeIsValid(int
timeUnit){
        if(timeUnit <= 0){
            throw new
IllegalArgumentException("Time Unit can't
be <= 0. Value passed in: " + timeUnit);
        }
    }
}
```
We're better off creating three small
methods, nowPlusMonths, nowPlusWeeks,
and nowPlusDays. This should work because

if you want a week and a half, you can just use nowPlusDays, 10 days, for example. So we split up the method and improved the code in two ways. First, we have small reusable methods with just a single simple argument, and the second benefit is that the number isn't magic anymore because it is clearly related to the method name, 4 days from now. Normally, we put magic numbers in a variable with a descriptive name, but if we have a method with a good name and a single argument, we don't need to do that. Is there a downside to what we did? Yes, we produced duplicate code. So now our code is WET and not DRY, and we'll fix that when we talk about code duplication later on. For now, let's focus on another example where we have too many arguments.

```
package m5methods;
public class
MethodWithTooManyArguments2 {
   public static void main(String[] args){
      String greeting = new
EmailSender().constructTemplateEmail("Mr.", "John", "Smith");
      Person john = new Person("Mr.",
"John", "Smith");
      String greeting2 = new
EmailSender().constructTemplateEmail(john);
//       new Person.Builder()
//          .title("Mr.")
//          .name("John")
//          .surname("Smith")
//          .build();
   }
   static class Person {
      String title;
      String name;
```

```java
        String surname;
        Person(String title, String name, String
surname) {
            this.title = title;
            this.name = name;
            this.surname = surname;
        }
        String getTitle() {
            return title;
        }
        String getName() {
            return name;
        }
        String getSurname() {
            return surname;
        }
    }
    static class EmailSender{
        String constructTemplateEmail(String
title, String name, String surname){
            return String.format("Dear %s %s
%s", title, name, surname);
        }
        String constructTemplateEmail(Person
person){
            String title = person.getTitle();
            String name = person.getName();
            String surname =
person.getSurname();
            // populate email template with the
args
            return String.format("Dear %s %s
%s", title, name, surname);
        }
    }
}
```

This EmailSender method takes three
strings, a title, a name, and a surname,
supposedly so that you can insert those into

some kind of a template and say Dear Mr. John Smith or something. These three strings could and should be encapsulated into a class, so we create a Person class with these fields. Then we create a Person object and then pass in that object as a single argument. And then inside that method, we call the getter methods. So again, the method has become much easier. We just pass in one single Person object inside of it and that's it. In this somewhat artificial example, you could argue that we just moved the problem elsewhere. Now we have a constructor with multiple arguments, but that can be fixed with either a builder pattern that I mentioned in the previous module or other ways. If you get such details from a database, you would build your Person object in a different way using some kind of framework anyway. So as you can see, there is more than one way to reduce the number of arguments, but it always depends on the context how you should approach reducing that number.

Flag Arguments

In the previous chapter, I mentioned that you might have too many arguments, and one of those arguments is a Boolean. These Boolean parameters are also called flag arguments, and long story short, you should avoid them. To quote Robert Martin, "Flag arguments are ugly. It immediately complicates the signature of the method, loudly proclaiming that this function does more than one thing. " I can't say that this should be regarded as some absolute rule, but more often than not, your code is better off without Boolean arguments. The most typical solution is to split the method.

```
switchLights(room, true);                          switchLightsOn(room);
                                    Split

                                                   switchLightsOff(room);
void switchLights(Room room,
                  boolean on){

    if(on){ // ... }

    else { // ... }
}
```

Now I might sound like a broken record. I keep saying that splitting the method into smaller pieces is a solution for this and that, but that's because it's true. Instead of having a single switchLights, create switchLightsOn and switchLightsOff.

Magic Numbers

Magic numbers are numbers whose purpose isn't obvious, and that's the case with the vast majority of numbers. they are particularly mysterious when they are passed in as parameters. If your method accepts numbers, then try to make it the only argument. Then the number is usually self-explanatory, not always, but frequently. And if you absolutely have to pass in multiple numbers, then please follow the guidelines of good variable naming and assign your number to a variable with a nice descriptive name, a simple thing to do, but somehow it gets neglected all the time.

Fail Fast

Now let's dive inside the method. We'll start of with code that you typically find at the top of the method, so we'll begin with the concept of failing fast. As the name suggests, with the fail-fast principle, you simply immediately report any failure that is likely to lead to another failure. This is the opposite of failsafe, which means you try to keep the show going, which in turn, often means that the system will crash anyway, just in a weird state that is difficult to analyze. So what are the benefits of failing fast? The main reason is faster debugging and troubleshooting, sometimes much faster. Let's take this method with some calculations as an example.

```
package m5methods;
public class FailFast {
    public static void main(String[] args) {
        int total =
getTotalCompensation(0);
        System.out.println(total);
    }
    private static int
getTotalCompensation(int
someBonusVariable) {
        if (someBonusVariable <= 0) {
            throw new
IllegalArgumentException("variable can't
be < 0 ");
        }
        int intermediateResult =
getBaseSalary() * someBonusVariable;
```

```
            int secondIntermediateResult =
convertToLocalCurrency(intermediateResul
t);
            return getSomeOtherMetric() /
secondIntermediateResult;
    }
    private static int
convertToLocalCurrency(int
intermediateResult) {
            return intermediateResult * 2;
    }
    private static int getSomeOtherMetric()
{
            return 5;
    }
    private static int getBaseSalary() {
            return 1000;
    }
}
```

I've just made them up, so it doesn't matter
what they do, but what does matter is if I run
this, I will get an arithmetic exception. This
is because on this line, I end up dividing by a
0, and I had to spend some time investigating
before I realized that a 0 was passed as an
argument. Maybe that shouldn't happen. But
to protect ourselves, we could save time
investigating all of this code and just throw
an IllegalArgumentException right at the
beginning. We might still need to think about
how we prevent 0 being passed here in the
first place, but this is already an
improvement. Run this code again, and it
still fails, obviously, but this time, much
earlier with a specific exception and a useful
message. We could add the same argument
check to our time methods. If we want to add
some days or weeks to the current time, then
0 or lower doesn't really make sense. Setting

an expiration time in the past actually sounds like a bug to me. And it's not just 0. We could check for nulls, for empty strings, or anything we need. All preconditioned check largely boil down to IllegalArgumentChecks and IllegalStateChecks. Preconditioned checks is such a widespread practice that multiple implementations exist.

Use Libraries :

- Native Java
  - - Objects.isNull();
- Guava
  - - Preconditions.checkArgument( );
- Apache
  - - ObjectUtils.isNotEmpty();

Native Java, Google's Guava libraries, and also, Apache utils all ship with a lot of helper methods that do such checks. What you see on the screen is just a single example from each. It goes without saying that all of them have many more, so feel free to use them. This way, you won't have to write that boilerplate if logic yourself.

Return Early

```
package m5methods;
public class ReturnEarly {
   private boolean systemIsUp;
   // Before
   public String getPersonalInfo(Person person, int pin){
      if (systemIsUp){
```

```java
        if (person != null &&
person.getName().equals("")){
            if(person.getPin() != pin){
                return  "Invalid pin";
            }
            return "Invalid Name";
        }
        return "System is down at the
moment";
    }
    return person.getPersonalInfo();
  }
  // After
  public String getPersonalInfo2(Person
person, int pin){
    if(!systemIsUp) return "System is down
at the moment";
    if(person != null &&
person.getName().equals("")) return
"Invalid Name";
    if(person.getPin() != pin) return
"Invalid pin";
    return person.getPersonalInfo();
  }
}
```

After we have made sure that the values of
our arguments are valid, we might write
some if-else logic, such as the one you see on
the screen. Multiple nested if statements lead
to high cyclomatic complexity, and it's
difficult to keep all those conditions in your
head. I mean, if you're reading this code, by
the time you get to the first return statement,
you have three conditions that you need to
keep in your own memory and analyze the
code at the same time, which is quite
difficult. Also, it's quite difficult to map
which if statement relates to which return
statement. To avoid this, we simply need to

check for simple conditions first and return immediately, like in the second version of the same method here. This approach has multiple benefits. If I see a return statement, I know I don't have to keep these conditions in mind anymore as I continue reading the code. And the second, conditions and return statements are visually mapped by simply being located on the same line. And last, but not least, overall, we have less lines of code. So if you have argument values that are valid, but they logically allow you to stop execution early, then evaluate these first and exit the function right away.

Refactor Duplication

Okay, so we validated the arguments in one case, and we returned early in another. After that comes the rest of the method body, and then here, we can do all sorts of things. But the focus of this chapter is whatever you do, make sure it's DRY. If you see duplication within the same method or you see duplication between two methods, consider extracting that duplicate piece of code into a separate method. Remember, smaller methods mean easier, flexible, and reusable code.

```java
package m5methods;
import java.time.LocalDateTime;
import java.time.ZoneId;
import static java.time.LocalDateTime.now;
public class
MethodWithTooManyArguments {
    public static void main(String[] args){
```

```
      new
Order().setExpirationDate(nowPlusDays(4));
   }
   public static long nowPlusMonths(int
months){
      checkTimeIsValid(months);
      return
toEpochMilli(now().plusMonths(months));
   }
   public static long nowPlusWeeks(int
weeks){
      checkTimeIsValid(weeks);
      return
toEpochMilli(now().plusWeeks(weeks));
   }
   public static long nowPlusDays(int days){
      checkTimeIsValid(days);
      return
toEpochMilli(now().plusDays(days));
   }
   private static long
toEpochMilli(LocalDateTime time){
      return
time.atZone(ZoneId.systemDefault())
         .toInstant()
         .toEpochMilli();
   }
   private static void checkTimeIsValid(int
timeUnit){
      if(timeUnit <= 0){
         throw new
IllegalArgumentException("Time Unit can't
be <= 0. Value passed in: " + timeUnit);
      }
   }
}
```

Let's take our methods that get us a point in time in the future. We did a good job by splitting the original big method, but that resulted in duplicated code. We repeat the same operation over and over, converting a LocalDateTime object to a primitive long value. We could extract that to a single place, so let's define a private static method that accepts the LocalDateTime object. It needs to accept it in order to convert it. We'll call the argument time, and all we do is repeat the conversion operation. Now we can use this method inside other methods. Come to think of it, we have this argument check duplicated, so how about wrapping it into a separate method as well? Let's call this method something like checkTimeIsValid that does this simple if verification. Now we can call this method from inside all other methods. So there we are, shorter, and it reads more like human language and not a programming language.

Conditionals

Conditionals simply convey if something is true or false, so they give you one option out of two. That sounds simple enough, yet there are still many ways how to write it in a non-clean way or make it confusing. One of the best ways to demonstrate an idea is to show an incremental example.
if (!doorClosed == false)
if (!doorClosed)
if (!isDoorClosed)
if (isDoorOpen)
So let's start with one of the most frequent bad habits, which is comparing a Boolean to true or false keywords. You don't need to do this. This is completely redundant, so just

remove the comparison. This is better, but this doesn't follow the Boolean naming convention, so let's add the is prefix. Now this is readable, short, and compliant at the same time. Well, almost. One more guideline is don't be anti-negative. In real life, do you normally say, come on in, the door is not closed, or simply, come on in, the door is open? I would assume that simply saying that something is open is simpler. The same goes for code. Just say something is open, switched on, present, and so on. The last tip I'd like to share with you concerns complex conditionals. It's normal to have complex business rules, and as such, complex validations. So you might end up with a complex statement, such as this.

```java
package m5methods;
import java.time.LocalTime;
public class ComplexConditional {
    public static void main(String[] args){
        int hour = getHourOfDay();
        if(hour > 6 && hour < 22){
            // day time logic
        } else {
            // night time logic
        }
    }
}
```

What we really want here is just a logical explanation of what we're trying to evaluate.

```java
package m5methods;
import java.time.LocalTime;
public class ComplexConditional {
    public static void main(String[] args){
        int hour = getHourOfDay();
        if(isDay(hour)){
            // day time logic
        } else {
```

```
    // night time logic
    }
  }
  private static boolean isDay(int hour){
    return hour > 6 && hour < 22;
  }
  private static int getHourOfDay() {
    return LocalTime.now().getHour();
  }
}
```

So the answer to this problem is extract it to a separate method that sounds like a true/false question and returns a Boolean. Now when I read the code, I can quickly understand what the code is trying to validate and move on inside the if block.

Ternary Expressions

I must say that ternary operations are great, and they are also evil. The guideline how to write good ternary operations is quite simple. Don't make them nested. Ternary operations are very useful one-liners.

```
String getTitle(Person p) {
return p.gender == Person.MALE ? "Mr. " : "Mrs. ";
}
```

For example, what you see is short and easy to understand. It's just one of the two options.

```
String getTitle(Person p) {
return p.gender == Person.MALE ? "Mr.":
p.isMarried() ? "Mrs.":"Miss";
}
```

However, whenever logic becomes more complicated, don't make the ternary operation itself more complicated.

Personally, I find even this simple example already a bit confusing. And here, I need to mentally draw arrows that go from one place to another as I try to find the right place to stop.

```
String getTitle(Person p) {
   if (p.gender == Person.MALE) {
      return "Mr.";
   }
   return p.isMarried() ? "Mrs." : "Miss";
}
```

Instead, consider changing it to a pure if-else statement or a mix of if statements and a simple ternary operation. Yes, this is more lines of code, but programming is not a competition about how much logic you can stuff into a single line. Clean code is about readability. Sometimes it means less lines of code, and this example shows that the opposite can also be true.

Summary

- Clean code concepts – DRY, CYC, Signal vs. Noise
- What to return & number of arguments
- Fail fast & return early
- Working with booleans

This was a fairly large module, and we covered a lot of ground, so let's do a recap. First, we had a quick overview of clean code concepts such as DRY, cyclomatic complexity, and signal to noise, and why they are important. We then moved on to method signature and saw how returning the right type and having the right set of arguments reduces complexity, which in turn, means cleaner code. After that, we discussed why failing fast and returning early at the very start of some methods may prove beneficial, and we saw how that worked in practice by refactoring some methods. Finally, we covered how conditional statements and operations should be handled in a clean, non-confusing manner. Complex conditionals deserve their own methods, and ternary operations should be kept simple.

Module 6 : Handling Exceptions

Introduction

As we all know, things can go wrong inside a program, and it definitely happens more often than we'd like to. Because it happens quite often, we also write exception handling code quite a lot, and this is why this book has a separate module on exceptions. The topic is big enough to deserve its own module. So exception handling, when used properly can improve a program's reliability and maintainability, but when used improperly, they can have the opposite effect. It could cause bugs that are much more difficult to investigate and it can clutter up the code so

much that you don't know anymore what the code is actually supposed to do.
- **Catching the wrong exceptions**
- **Ignoring exceptions**
- **Useless code in catch block**
- **Exceptions in finally block**

So in this module, we are going to talk about best practices surrounding exception handling, why you shouldn't try and catch all possible exceptions, why you shouldn't ignore exceptions, and how you can balance between the two. To be honest, this is a very short list. The topic of exception handling is much wider, but I want to stay focused and give you just the most essential guidelines, so I've picked the most frequent and important exception handling issues that can be encountered.

Catch Specific Exceptions

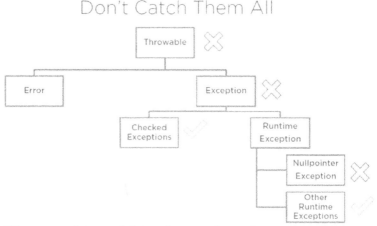

There are lots and lots of exceptions, but before we talk about how to handle them, let's first talk about what exceptions we shouldn't handle in the first place. So first, don't catch the top-level throwable because you might catch errors, such as out of memory error or internal error. And you are not meant to even try and recover from such events, so please don't do it. Next, try to avoid catching the general exception as well, at least 90% of the time. Why? Because you might catch some runtime exceptions that shouldn't be caught. You have to somehow handle checked exceptions, so there is not much to discuss there, but there are some runtime exceptions that shouldn't be handled. And one worth highlighting is the NullPointerException. NullPointers aren't supposed to be caught because they are usually the result of programming errors. So if we catch and handle NullPointers, then we essentially cover up our own programming mistakes, a bit like sweeping problems under the carpet. That's not a good thing. Instead, try your best to prevent nulls as much as possible, especially if it's in your own code. But sometimes you have no control whether you get a null from some third-party software, so then the second best thing you can do is check for null with an if statement.

```java
package m6exceptions;
import java.io.FileNotFoundException;
import java.io.IOException;
import java.sql.SQLException;
public class MultipleExceptions {
   public static void main(String[] args){
      // too long
      try {
         readFile();
         executeSqlQuery();
      } catch (FileNotFoundException ex) {
         // handle it!
```

```java
    } catch (IOException e) {
      // handle it!
    } catch (SQLException e) {
      // handle it!
    }
    // NO!
    try {
      readFile();
      executeSqlQuery();
    } catch (Exception ex) {
      // one exception to rule them all!
    }
    try {
      readFile();
      executeSqlQuery();
    } catch (IOException | SQLException
ex) {
      // balance - handle it Java 7 way
    }
    // NO!
    try {
      readFile();
      executeSqlQuery();
    } catch (IOException | SQLException
ex) {
      if (ex instanceof IOException) {
        // ...
      }
      if (ex instanceof SQLException){
        // ...
      }
    }
  }
  private static void executeSqlQuery()
throws SQLException {
    throw new SQLException();
  }
  private static void readFile()throws
IOException {
```

```
      throw new IOException();
   }
}
```

Let's take a look at an example when you might be tempted to catch a top-level exception. Over here, we have a try block that invokes one or two methods, and together, they throw multiple exceptions. So you write several catch blocks until you end up with a long list, and you start to get the feeling that this isn't right. You have just a few lines of code that do the actual work and then double the amount of code that tries to catch something. What people tend to do as a countermeasure is just catch one single general exception. As you can see, this is much less code so it looks like clean code; however, it is not advised to do this. As I've said, the problem with this approach is that you might end up catching unwanted runtime exceptions, such as NullPointer, and we have already discussed that we should prevent them. So what do we do? Revert back to this ugly, long catching chain? If you want to handle each exception differently, then yes. Why not? But if you're happy to handle all of them or some of them in the same way, then Java 7 or later has you covered. You can declare all of them in a single line, like so, and separate them using a vertical bar. The benefit is fewer lines of code. The downside is that you can't tailor your exception message for each. You have to write a more generic message that fits them all. Just don't start branching code with if statements like you see on the screen because that doesn't bring any benefit compared to the original way of doing it. If you are tempted to do this because you want to have a specific message for each exception, then you might as well just have a long catch list.

Catch Block

Catch Block Anti-patterns :
Catch block shouldn't:
- Be empty
- Have only comments
- Contain unhelpful code
Multiple AntiPattern exist when it comes to catch blocks, but the top three most frequent offenders are empty blocks, blocks that have only comments when the exceptions could have been at least logged, and finally, the nonobvious action of filling it up with useless code.

```
catch {                                         }    ✗
catch { // should never happen                  }    ✗
catch { return null;                            }    ✗
catch { e.printStackTrace();                    }    ✗
catch { log.error(e);                           }    ✓
catch { throw new CustomException(e);           }    ✓
```

If you have seen empty catch blocks in other people's code, please don't consider this the norm. It's not. The catch block exists on purpose for a reason. So don't leave it empty and don't add comments saying something like this should never happen. Because ironically, the things that should never happen actually do so very often. Leaving comments without any proper action is essentially hiding, or I should even say, obfuscating the problem, and the only outcome of that is a longer debugging session. Also, just a reminder, don't return null. We talked about return types in the previous module. Ignoring exceptions is bad, but filling it up with code that isn't helpful is, well, not helpful either.

```
package m6exceptions;
public class ExceptionHandling {
   public static void main(String[] args){
      try {
         isAdult(-1);
      } catch (IllegalArgumentException ex) {
         ex.printStackTrace();
      }
   }
   private static void isAdult(int age) throws
IllegalArgumentException{
      if( age < 0){
         throw new
IllegalArgumentException("Invalid age");
      }
   }
}
```

Take this piece of code that forms an illusion of handling the exception properly and is using a method printStackTrace. If you run this code, then you see in the console, a simple stack trace, an exception, and some message defined in that exception.

```
package m6exceptions;
public class ExceptionHandling {
   public static void main(String[] args){
         isAdult(-1);
      try {
      } catch (IllegalArgumentException ex) {
         ex.printStackTrace();
```

```
        }
    }
    private static void isAdult(int age) throws
IllegalArgumentException{
        if( age < 0){
            throw new
IllegalArgumentException("Invalid age");
        }
    }
}
```

Okay. Now let's move this method outside the try block and run the code again. Do you see any difference in terms of useful information? No, because there isn't any. So printing the stack trace or the message of the code exception doesn't do anything extra. We should have that information anyway. What you want to do instead is log the exception using a logging framework. So what are the useful things to do inside a catch block? Mostly, two things. First log it using a logging framework. I have already mentioned that a moment ago. And second, just rethrow it and pass all useful information to the exception. Let's see what I mean by useful information. Over here, we have a stack trace saying Invalid age. That's not bad, but it can be better.

```
package m6exceptions;
public class ExceptionHandling {
    public static void main(String[] args){
        try {
//          isAdult(-1);
            isAdult2(-1);
        } catch (IllegalArgumentException ex) {
            ex.printStackTrace();
        }
    }
```

```java
    private static void isAdult(int age) throws
IllegalArgumentException{
    if( age < 0){
        throw new
IllegalArgumentException("Invalid age");
    }
}
    private static void isAdult2(int age) throws
IllegalArgumentException{
    if( age < 0){
        // or custom IllegalAgeException
        throw new
IllegalArgumentException("The age should
be at least 0. Actual age value passed: " +
age);
    }
}
}
```

I will now improve the exception message, and now I run the same piece of code again. There. The age should be at least 0, actual age value passed -1. That gives us much more information right from the start. The condition that must be met and the value that failed that condition. So whatever causes the exception, try and pass that information into the exception message.

Finally Block

```java
package m6exceptions;
import java.io.File;
import java.io.FileNotFoundException;
import java.util.Scanner;
public class ExceptionInFinallyBlock {
    public static void main(String[] args){
        try {
```

```java
        int result = 1/0; //
ArithmeticException
    } finally {
        cleanup();
    }
  }
  private static void cleanup() {
     throw new IllegalStateException();
  }
  void readFile(){
     try (Scanner scanner = new
Scanner(new File("file.txt"))) {
        // read file
     } catch (FileNotFoundException e) {
        // handle it!
     }
  }
}
```

Until now, we have mostly talked about the try and catch blocks, but let's not forget there is also the finally block, and the main thing to remember about the finally block is to ensure that no exceptions should be thrown inside of it or at least you should prevent it from escaping. Why? Well, the easiest way to explain is to show. Here I have a try block, and inside, I try and do a mathematical operation. If that fails, I'm trying to do some cleanup in the finally block. Let's run this and see what happens, and it fails with an exception, but not the one that we expected. The try block throws an arithmetic exception. And this is what we should have seen, but then it got masked, in other words, hidden by the second exception from the finally block. So the real reason why a program failed is exception A, but we got presented with exception B. This is something that really hurts investigation. So do your best to avoid methods that throw exceptions in the finally block. You could try and catch it as well, but then we get nested exception handling, and we don't want that. It can get a bit messy. As a reminder, if you have Java 7 or higher, then prefer try-with-resources statement, which can handle cleanup for you. For example, if you try and open a file and you get an I/O exception, then closing that resource is done for you by Java itself.

Summary

- Catch specific exceptions
- Proper handling in catch { }
- Finally block and Java 7 try-with-resources

Let's do a quick recap. We have seen what kind of exceptions we shouldn't catch. If we do, what kind of practices we should avoid in our catch block and how to write cleaner code if we decide to catch multiple exceptions. Last, but not least, we have seen that we can accidentally hide the real problem in the finally block, as well as the possibility to avoid it altogether if we use the Java 7 try-with-resources mechanism. This has been a relatively short module, giving it just the most essential tips and guidelines when it comes to exception handling.

Module 7 : Class Organization

Introduction

This time we're going to take a step back and talk about classes. So far, we have been talking about one thing at a time, just variables and their names, or just constructors, or just methods and what happens inside of them. So if we take care of each individual piece, then the sum, your entire software should be clean as well, right? Well, yes and no. If you follow practices that we have discussed until now, your code should be in good shape, but that doesn't mean there is no more room for improvement. And sometimes you need to take a step back and inspect how all of the individual pieces are put together, and whether they form a coherent logical picture. So in this module, let's zoom out a little bit, and look at the class as a whole.

- **Revisit SRP**
- **Cohesion & Coupling**
- **Style Conventions**
- **Principle of Proximity**

We'll first briefly revisit the single responsibility principle and follow up with the concept of cohesion and coupling. We'll discuss what they mean to the size and content of a class. We'll then talk about Java style conventions that you should adhere to and why, as well as how formatting and even the order of code impacts it equality. We'll wrap up by looking at several things that you can study after this book to take your clean code skills to the next level.

SRP

So, the SRP or the single responsibility principle, something that has been debated and discussed on the internet for at least a decade, or more like multiple decades. This principle applies to both methods and classes. We apply the SRP to a method and split it into multiple smaller methods, so each one does one thing. But what about classes? Well, the SRP can be applied to classes as well, but it gets more complicated, meaning it becomes more vague and open to interpretation. Let's take a step back and look at the definition of the SRP in the context of classes.

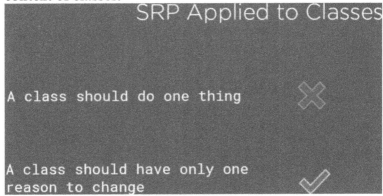

If you replace the word method with the word class, then you get the rule a class should do one thing. But that would result in terribly tiny classes doing almost nothing. A class with two methods would already break this rule, so that's misleading. Robert Martin defines SRP as a principle where a class should have one reason to change. And this is tricky because agreeing on the definition of the word responsibility is often subject to personal opinion. Nevertheless, I'll try and explain.

```
class SomeClass {
String field1;
String field2;
void doThingA()
void doThingB()
void doUnrelatedThing()
}
```

Imagine you have this class with a bunch of fields and methods. Imagine that the code is super clean. We apply the naming principles and refactor the entire class and methods. So each individual snippet could not be better. But when we look at it as a whole, some methods do something unrelated to the class. I mean, the methods are useful and they are used throughout the system, but they're misplaced. So if we apply the SRP principle, we should refactor those out into a separate class, essentially splitting.

```
class SomeClass {
   String field1;
   void doThingA()
   void doThingB()
}
class AnotherClass {
   String field2;
   void doUnrelatedThing()
}
```

And you might think can I get at least one specific example, and the answer is yes. Let's take a look at this Employee class.

```
class Employee {
    String getName()
    double getSalary()
    Role getRole()
    void sendEmail()
    void calculateYearBonus()
}
```

An employee has a name, a salary, and a role, for example, developer, tester, manager, and so on. What do most office employees do? They send email, and in my opinion, a bit too frequently, but in a big organization, that's just life. And the company also has yearly bonuses, so we have a calculation method. We would create an employee object and invoke this method on that specific employee. However, from a technical perspective, the employee is not the one who sends the email, it's an email service, for example, Microsoft Outlook that does the sending. And employees don't calculate their own bonuses, I mean, I would love that, but it's another department's responsibility to do this. So in the end, we should split this into three classes.

```
class Employee {
    // getter methods
}
class EmailService {
    void sendEmail()
}
class PayrollCalculator {
    void calculateYearBonus(Employee emp)
}
```

This way, each class has a separate technical functional scope, but not just that, each class is now a separate unit from a business perspective. Employee would belong to the domain of human resources, email service to the IT administration, and payroll calculation belongs to accounts. Now a word about role-based separation. In his blog, Robert Martin gives a solid explanation about how he applies the SRP and asks the question who and not what to decide what functionality he puts into any given class. So, another thing is that adhering to SRP naturally leads to higher cohesion, and we'll talk about cohesion next.

Cohesion

So, I have said that SRP leads to higher cohesion, and that is a good thing. And if you're not entirely sure what that really means, now is a good time to gain a deeper understanding. Cohesion in general context simply means a tendency to unite, meaning things are grouped or logically connected together. So cohesion happens when things put together make sense and work well. If you take all of the separate parts of a car and put them together, you get a functional car, that's cohesive. If you want a police car, you might add a siren on top of that. That's still cohesive. However, would you stick an anchor behind it to serve as an extra break system? Probably not, and that's not cohesive. So in the context of programming, cohesion refers to the degree to which the elements inside a class or a module belong together. To achieve high cohesion inside a class, we should keep related things, fields, and methods together.
Cohesive Class :
- Fields and methods are co-dependent

- Methods that use multiple class fields indicate higher cohesion
- Methods use other methods inside the same class

So high cohesion means that the glass is focused on what it should be doing, meaning fields and methods are codependent and hang together as a logical whole, and they all relate to the intention of the class. How do we achieve high cohesion? By making sure that the methods are interrelated and they use the class fields. If a method uses three or four class fields, that's higher cohesion than just one field. Typically you achieve higher cohesion in smaller focused classes, and right now you might be thinking to yourself, this is the SRP slide, so are you just telling me the same thing, but using different terminology? The answer to that is no. SRP and cohesion go hand in hand, but they are not the same thing. You can have a highly-cohesive class, which is a good thing, but that class still might have multiple responsibilities, which is a bad thing. Let's look at this example.

Cohesive but Not SRP :

```
User user;
void saveChanges(){
    dbContext.save();
    logger.log("User table updated with: " +
whatever);
    raiseEvent(new EmailNotification(user));
}
void raiseEvent(Event event){
    // ...
};
```

We have a field and two methods all inside a single class. We trigger saveChanges, we delegate the saving to a database context, that's fine, then we'll log it, that's also fine, and then we send a notification email that a new user has been created. Notice how one method uses another method, and the other method uses the class field. There are various issues with this code, but one could argue that the code is interconnected functionally, and thus is cohesive. But, saving to a database and sending emails are definitely two different responsibilities. So the SRP is broken at method level, it does two things, and also at class level. The event raising should be part of a different class. It's quite difficult to think of an example that would distinguish SRP and cohesion in a clear and simply way, but I hope this helps. Cohesion at Different Levels :

- Class
- Package
- Module
- Systems

One more thing to note about cohesion is that it doesn't only happen at class level. We talked about it in the context of a class, but it should be respected at higher levels. For example, at package level, don't just dump all of your classes in a single package. Group them into multiple packages. The same then applies to modules or subsystems. The interaction between these should be logical and ordered.

Coupling

Coupling is another concept that frequently gets mentioned together with cohesion. In simple words, it is the degree of interdependence between software modules or classes, a measure of how interconnected they are or how much one class or a component knows about the details of the other.

```
public class A {
    private B b = new B(); // A coupled with B
}
```

As the most simple example, if you have class A that uses class B, then A is coupled with B, that's it, that's coupling. A is dependent on B to work correctly. Obviously in practically any object-oriented program, coupling is completely fine, it's not something you need or can avoid. But there are degrees of coupling, very loose, very tight, and everything in between. And usually you want it as loose as possible. Why? Because tight coupling means classes or modules are so tight that you cannot change one without changing the other. And loose coupling means that a change in one class requires no or minimum changes in another class. So with loose coupling, if you think you need to change one line, you really do change one line. With tight coupling, you change one line, and suddenly you see yourself forced and change much more in 20 other related classes. Which brings us to the simple conclusion that tight coupling is maintenance hell, and clean code isn't just readable, it's also maintainable. So high cohesion and low coupling allow for better maintenance. Okay, so how do you reduce coupling?

To Reduce Coupling :
- **Adhere to SRP**
- **Increase Cohesion**

- **Program to an Interface**
- **Maintain strong Encapsulation**
- **Use Dependency Injection**

You reduce coupling by adhering to the SRP principle and increasing cohesion. One big class will be coupled to 10 different classes, but 5 small classes might be coupled with only two classes each. But that's not the only thing you can do. The most frequent advice to reduce coupling is to program to an interface. And there's a good reason for that. You may have heard about this guideline, but let's take a look at a few examples.

```
public class CouplingExample1 {
    // Not programming to an Interface
    LinkedList<String> list = new
LinkedList<>();
    void doSomething(LinkedList<String>
list){
        String firstElem = list.getFirst();
        // do something with firstElem
    }
    void
doSomethingElse(LinkedList<String> list){
        String lastElem = list.getLast();
        // do something with lastElem
    }
}
```

So first, let's look at the class example of using lists. We started off with a linked list, and then we use it in two different methods, one gets the first element and does something with it, and the other gets the last element. Notice that we use the methods getFirst and getLast because they are present on LinkedList. Now, let's change our minds and decide that we want an array list.

```
public class CouplingExample1 {
```

```java
// Not programming to an Interface
ArrayList<String> list = new
ArrayList<>();
void doSomething(ArrayList<String>
list){
    String firstElem = list.get(0);
    // do something with firstElem
}
    void doSomethingElse(ArrayList<String>
list){
    String lastElem = list.get(list.size() - 1);
    // do something with lastElem
}
}
```

Notice that I have to change it in one, two, three, four places. That's a lot, but let's proceed anyway. And now this code doesn't compile because the array list doesn't have these magic getFirst and getLast methods. So that's two extra changes, so now we have a total of six places needed to change in this one tiny, simple class. I mean, all of this code fits on one screen, and it all has to change. Imagine a piece of software with 1000 classes. You might end up spending an entire day trying to make your changes work just because you didn't program to an interface from the start.

```java
public class CouplingExample1 {
    // Programming to an Interface
    List<String> list2 = new LinkedList<>();
    void doSomething2(List<String> list){
        String firstElem = list.get(0);
        // do something with firstElem
    }
    void doSomethingElse2(List<String> list){
        String lastElem = list.get(list.size() - 1);
        // do something with lastElem
    }
```

```
}
```

Now this is the alternative scenario. We start off by creating a new LinkedList again, but this time the type is just a list, an interface. Now the other two methods accept the list interface and are forced to work with the get methods that are declared in that interface.

```
public class CouplingExample1 {
    // Programming to an Interface
    List<String> list2 = new ArrayList<>();
    void doSomething2(List<String> list){
        String firstElem = list.get(0);
        // do something with firstElem
    }
    void doSomethingElse2(List<String> list){
        String lastElem = list.get(list.size() - 1);
        // do something with lastElem
    }
}
```

And now if I change the LinkedList to an ArrayList, I change it in just one place, everything else stays the same. This is the power of programming to an interface. When you decide to swap A for B, you can either change it in one place in 5 seconds, or in the entire program, taking up half a day. Let's quickly take a look at another coupling example.

```
import java.io.File;
import java.io.InputStream;
public class CouplingExample2 {
    public int calculateSomething(File source){
        //open InputStream from File
        return 0;
    }
    public int calculateSomething2(InputStream source){
        //read from InputStream
```

```
        return 0;
    }
}
```

Over here we have a method that does some calculations, and it needs some data to perform the task. As you can see, it takes a file, so we have a dependency on the file class. Not only that, we are essentially coupled to the local file system. If someone comes over and says hey, can we give you data from a database, the answer is no, sorry, I'm tightly coupled to the file object. Hmm, okay, can we send you the data over HTTP from a web service? The answer is again no, sorry, I have this tight dependency on this one thing. Of course, alternatively you create additional methods, each with a unique implementation. And here's the other method that takes an ImputStream, and the ImputStream can be obtained from a file, a database, or a URL connection. So the number of dependencies is the same, one, but we suddenly have much more flexibility. This doesn't guarantee that you can now accept input from all possible sources, but it goes to show that choosing the wrong type from the start can drastically reduce flexibility, and choosing the right option keeps a high-level of flexibility for the future. One more thing that helps loose coupling and requires little effort is to maintain strong encapsulation. By that I mean keep things as private as possible.

Stronger Encapsulation :

```
public class A {
    private String a; // for internal use only
    private String b;
    public void doSomething(){
        doAnotherThing();
```

```
}

    public void doAnotherThing(){ //... }
    public String getA() { return a;}
}
```

Look at this class, it has private fields and public methods, and everything seems fine. However, that second method(doAnotherThing) is only used internally by the first method. And if that's the case, it shouldn't be public. Why? Because someone might use it in another class, thus creating unnecessary coupling. So let's make it private. How about that public getA method? Public getter methods are extremely common, but that doesn't mean we should create them for everything. The field String A is meant to be used internally, so it shouldn't be exposed. In this case, we can simply remove the entire method. Less code and less coupling with other classes. So to repeat, don't make methods and fields public just because. You should do the exact opposite, make everything as private as possible. You have no idea how others will use your code, so expose only the necessary bits. Last, but not least, I would like to mention the concept of dependency injection. This practice also allows for greater software maintainability, but it's a large non-trivial topic, and it's outside the scope of this book.

Module Recap

We have covered a lot of ground, and I would like to do a quick half-way recap to be sure we're not lost. We have seen that SRP means that you should create small focused classes with a single responsibility. We have seen that this leads to cohesion, meaning we should group logically and functionally similar things together. And finally, we talked about coupling and how we should keep it loose. So, adhere to SRP, keep cohesion high, and coupling low. All of these principles contribute to greater flexibility. This makes the code easier and faster to change, so they mostly contribute to maintainability. And clean code is both readable and maintainable. For the rest of this module, we're going to talk about readability again.

Style Conventions

Style conventions is probably one of the most boring topics out there, so it gets neglected quite a lot. Nevertheless, I will try and show you it's worth the time and effort. Have you ever thought that punctuation and overall grammar is a good thing, and it's great we learn it at school? Google has a Java Style Guide, and as you can see, they leave no stone unturned. Curly braces, indentation, line wrapping, everything matters, and I believe if Google software developers think it's important, then we should make an effort as well. As Twitter says on their GitHub page, their Java style guide is the distillation of many combined man-years of software engineering and Java development experience. I won't just read out loud how much space you should have between your lines of code or how you should place your curly braces, it's all very well documented, and you are free to read up on these things.

Principle of Proximity

One thing that deserves to be mentioned separately is the principle of proximity or the proximity rule. And it basically means that you should try and organize your code in a way that it reads like a book or a newspaper article, from top to bottom. Let me show you what I mean.

```
public class ProximityRule {
   void methodA(){
      methodB();
   }
   private void methodC() {
      doThatThing();
   }

   private void methodB() {
      methodC();
   }

   void doThatThing(){
   }
}
```

I need to understand this class. I start at the top, and I look at the first method. I see that it calls methodB, so I scroll down until I find it. This method invokes methodC, and now I spend my time searching for that method again. And then again I must continue with my scrolling journey, constantly going up and down. This is annoying. What if we had related methods placed one after the other?

Let me quickly place the methods in a different order.

```java
public class ProximityRule {
  void methodA(){
    methodB();
  }
  private void methodB() {
    methodC();
  }
  private void methodC() {
    doThatThing();
  }
  void doThatThing(){
  }
}
```

There, now if I start again, I'll look at the first method, I see methodB, and all I have to do is look a bit lower without scrolling or doing any other action. And as I continue inspecting code, I'm just reading from top to bottom, as if I'm reading a book. A quick reminder, spend the majority of our time reading code and thinking, so this little trick, placing interconnected methods in the right order really helps this activity. Applying the proximity rule requires almost no effort, it's super easy, but it makes a difference because it creates a very nice reading flow.

Further Material

- SRP
- Open Closed Principle
- Liskov Substitution Principle
- Interface Segregation Principle
- Dependency Inversion

We are almost done with this module. Frankly talking about clean code at class level and higher means talking about software design, and that's a huge learning area. So, before we finish this module, I'd like to briefly highlight further material for you to explore. You already know SRP, but this principle is not standalone. It's actually part of a larger group of principles called the SOLID principles. SRP, Open Closed Principle, Liskov Substitution Principle, interface-segregation principle, and finally dependency inversion principle. And I've actually already mentioned the last one, the dependency injection principle, which is based on dependency inversion.

Summary

- SRP, Cohesion and Coupling
- Style conventions
- Principle of Proximity

This module was packed with information, so let's review what we have learned. First we looked at the SRP principle, as well as cohesion and coupling. These concepts don't add that much to readability, but they certainly are important for maintainability. And as we know, clean code is about both. We then moved on to what makes code readable inside a class. And similar to normal text inside books, you want to have certain style and rules, and multiple known companies such as Google and Twitter openly publish their style guides. They are there for people to explore, and it's definitely worth reading. Finally, we have seen well-written methods don't necessarily lead to a well-organized class. You need to take your methods and the rest of your code inside a class, and apply the proximity rule, meaning you should order your code in such a way that it flows as naturally as possible from top to bottom. We have mostly talked about code that gets compiled and executed, but there is one more kind of code, and that's comments. Comments get ignored by the compiler, but as a human reading code, you also read them all the time. So let's see how comments can be good and evil, and what you should do about them.

Module 8 : Writing Comments

Introduction

This time we are going to talk about comments. If you write code, you most likely write comments as well. I certainly do, but I try to avoid comments as much as possible. Why? Because it's likely that in some cases, those comments are at best useless, but in many cases, they are actually more evil than good. And this is going to be the focus of this module, learning to recognize evil comments and how to fix them. First, let's understand why everyone writes comments.
Why We Write Comments :

- **Helps to understand code**
- **Express personal opinion**
- **Disable functionality**

We do so in belief that comments are good, they help other people understand what is going on in the code. That may be true, but it's often just a patch for poorly-written code. Second, comments may be used to literally express some personal opinion, which is plain useless. Actually it's clutter, meaning it's noise, and we want signal. Third, comments may be used to temporarily disable misbehaving code. Often that's even worse because it hides a problem that no one fixes for a long time. It can cause a cascade of hidden problems. For example, commented-out code covers up a bug, that covers up another bug, and fixing that uncovers yet another bug. Remember we talked about signal to noise ratio? Signal is clean and useful code, noise is everything else. If you think of all the ways comments are used, then I'd say comments mostly end up as noise. There is a huge number of comments out there that should be just removed without mercy.

- **Redundant comments**
- **Misleading comments**
- **Useless and misplaced comments**
- **Commented out code**
- **Legitimate comments**

So in this module, we're going to talk about redundant comments, comments that lie or mislead, comments that contain all kinds of information that shouldn't even be there, commented-out code, as well as legitimate situations and reasons for a good comment.

Compensating Comments

```
class Customer {
        String name; // customer name
        // get customer age
        int getAge(){
                return name;
        }
}
```

A redundant comment is simply a comment that doesn't add any useful information. It's basically what you see on the screen right now. You have a well-named variable and the method with a good, clear name. And then right next to them you have comments that say exactly the same thing. So name is the name of the customer, thank you for stating the obvious. GetAge gets you the age of the customer. I don't know where I'd be without that comment. The same goes for basic language constructs. Here you see a simple loop.

```
// loops over a list of books
for(Book book : books){
        if(book.getTitle().equals("Lord of The
        Rings")){
                return true;
        }
}
```

Is it clear what it does? Yes it is. This loop loops over a list of books and returns true if we find a specific title. So if we add comments, loops over a list of books, or return true if we find the right book, is that going to help? Is it going to increase our understanding? No, not at all. The code is super clear as is, so stating the obvious about loops, if statements, switch statements, or try catch blocks is entirely unnecessary because this is basic language syntax. All of this might seem obvious to you, I mean that redundant comments are redundant, yet somehow such comments can be found very frequently. So if you see them, simply remove them, they add no extra value, they are just additional words that you need to spend time reading.

Logs, Wikis and TODOs

The usage of comments is generally limited only by human imagination, and as such, programmers use comments for logging, fixes, and changes. For example, you can encounter a method and a large list of changes right above it. This list contains how this method had a bug and it was fixed, then another bullet point telling you that it was slow, but was optimized using some kind of caching, and so on, and so forth. If I read in code, I only want to see the latest version of it, and I should have a reasonable assumption that it works. If it doesn't and if there is a bug, then I simply look into the history of this file using version control. And I do hope that you use some kind of version control system at work, such as Git. If you don't, I can only highly recommend you start doing so. Additionally, people sometimes add a TODO comment to log technical debt. There is nothing wrong with a TODO in itself, sometimes you have to meet some deadline, but there is the right way and the wrong way to leave a TODO. We'll talk about the right way later, but here's a list of how not to leave a TODO. Just a TODO, this one's horrible, do what, with what, by whom, by when? No information given what so ever. TODO with a vague comment such as improve this code, what's wrong with this code? I have no idea. It just says Fix this. Fix what exactly, and again who and when should fix it? Finally, a TODO with commented out code, and that's another level of evil. I will talk about commented-out code separately in another chapter.

Misleading Comments

Comments aren't always just noise that can be simply removed. They can also be misleading or lie, and that is when they start being harmful. When I say lie, I don't mean that the person who wrote that comment did so on purpose. But code is changed frequently, however, comments are not. This happens with anything that is written twice. Something gets changed in one place, but not in the other, even if it's right next to it. So if code gets changed and comments don't, then they become outdated, which leads to a situation where they say one thing, and the code is doing another.

```
class Person {
        // Return data as a String
        PersonalData getPersonalData(){
                // ...
        }
}
```

For example, the initial implementation was returning a string, for example a JSON string, but developers changed their mind and decided to encapsulate personal information into a separate class, so the return type changed, but the comment just above it didn't. Now you're stuck reading and thinking, should I change the comments or the code? Now, you should believe code, but it's also a good idea to double check that the comment is indeed outdated, which means again wasting your time. But once you are sure that the comment is incorrect, don't update it, remove it instead. And if code is difficult to understand without it, then you know what to do, improve it.

Commented out Code

```
public String getPersonalInfo(Person person){
        // if (systemIsUp){ TODO
                return
        person.getPersonalInfo();
        // }
}
```
Now let's talk about the worst kind of comment, commented-out code without a proper explanation. There are two major reasons why commented-out code is bad. You can't just get rid of it, you don't know how important it is and what the consequences will be if you delete it. Of course the software functionality isn't going to change if you delete it because it's ignored anyway, but what if it's a critical piece? Now you need to investigate and hope that someone else knows. The alternative to deleting it is to uncomment it, but what

happens then? The entire program is at least 5 years old, and how can you be sure that it's not going to cascade throughout the entire system and cause all sorts of bugs and undesirable behavior. There might be an exceptional scenario where you need to very quickly fix a critical problem, but you should try and fix that first thing next day. But in most cases, commenting out code is such a terrible practice Please, please, please don't comment out code and then push it.

Useful Comments

That was a lot of talking about how comments are evil, but that doesn't mean that there are no legitimate use cases.
Good Comments :
- JavaDoc
- Compensate for factors outside of your control
- TODOs with an explainer or issue tracker number

The most obvious one is JavaDoc. The basic guideline is to have a JavaDoc on all public methods, especially if these methods are part of some library that it's widely used by others. This is because sometimes even if the method has a good name, it might execute some complex algorithm or you might want to learn more about the internals. Note that IDEs make it easy to create JavaDoc. In IntelliJ, for example, I can simply type /, the asterisk character twice, and hit Enter. And I immediately get a template that is ready to be filled in, so that's really convenient. One note about JavaDoc, it's not always necessary, for example, it doesn't add any informational value on basic getters and setters, such as Get day of week. It's self explanatory, so a JavaDoc telling you what it does and what it returns is redundant, at least here. So obvious JavaDoc is just as useless as a obvious comment. One more reason you might want to place a comment is when you have to write code to compensate for factors that are outside of your control. Two examples come to mind, using third-party software and unstable environments, and I experienced both. Essentially, if there's something bad or suboptimal that you cannot influence or change yourself directly, then you have to write suboptimal client code, and it's fine to add a comment for the next person saying yes, this is weird, but otherwise it's impossible because some other software we interact with does this and that. Last, but not least are the TODOs. Sometimes you need to complete a task, and you find that further nontrivial improvements could be made to some piece of code. So we can leave a TODO comment, but it should be a TODO comment that clearly answers the questions what needs to be done, why it needs to be done, and when it should be done. Even better, if your team uses some issue tracker, then just leave the ticket number next to that TODO, and of course place all useful information in that ticket. This is even because you can immediately prioritize and assign this ticket to someone on your team, so this TODO does not become eternal technical debt. From my personal experience, if you don't assign a specific task to a specific person, then you're not going to find many volunteers.

Summary

- Comments shouldn't compensate for bad code
- Obvious comments should be removed
- Useful comments

Comments, who would have thought that they could be used and misused in so many ways? But as we have seen, that is often the case. So let's recap. We have seen that comments are frequently used to compensate for bad code in one way or another. And the most frequent way to deal with them is to remove the comment and improve the code itself. We have also seen that obvious comments that give no extra information should be simply removed without any code changes because the only thing they do is waste your time by making you read them until you learn to ignore them. Finally, we have seen that comments do have a right to exist, and there's a range of valid use cases, going from useful and informative JavaDoc for public methods, to situations where you have to compensate for situations and software that you have to work with, but they are outside of your control.

Module 9 : Improving Tests

Introduction

It is widely accepted that writing tests is necessary for any nontrivial project. You might write only unit tests, or a range of functional integration, or UI tests. It doesn't matter which kind of test, but what's important is to treat the test code just like any other code, it should be clean. Although a lot of guidelines are the same for test and application code, some are different, or they have different priorities. Entire books and courses exist on how to write tests, and the aim of this module is not to duplicate that effort, but to highlight the most important principles that you should follow.

- DAMP Principle
- Focused Tests
- Test Template

So in this module, we're going to talk about the DAMP principle, the benefit of keeping your tests focused, and following some kind of test format template, such as AAA or BDD style.

DAMP Tests

So, you remember that DRY stands for Don't Repeat Yourself. In practice, this means refactoring any kind of duplication. And the opposite of that is WET, which stands for Write Everything Twice. And we also know that your application code should be as DRY and possible, unless it starts hurting readability; however, DRY is not the most important principle in tests. What really matters in tests is the balance between DRY and WET, and it's called, wait for it, DAMP. And I'm not making this up. DAMP stands for Descriptive and Meaningful Phrases, which simply means that you should strive for maximum readability in your tests, even if it means some amount of duplication. DAMP does not promote mindless copy/pasting, it promotes a balance between readability and duplication. But why is duplication more acceptable in tests? Reasons for Duplication in Tests :
- Multiple tests may test the same function
- Very DRY test code may:
    - Be less readable
    - Become too complex (tests should be simple)

Well, tests often verify the same thing, for example, you could have five tests for one single public method, and the only thing that varies is one or two inputs. However, unlike production code, this duplication is usually isolated in that single test class. Because of this, the duplication is minimal and obvious.

But what if I remove this duplication anyway and make my test as DRY as possible? Then you might reduce the test readability. Less readable means more difficult to maintain. And the number one reason for tests being thrown out the window is that they take too much effort to maintain. Also, if you follow the DRY principle too much, you could potentially make your test code complex enough that it might need testing as well. If you find yourself wanting to write test code for test code, then that's a sure sign you want to just simplify your tests. It takes some time and practice to find the right balance, but if you're unsure, ask yourself can I glance through this test code and understand what it's trying to achieve, what it's trying to verify? So to summarize, favor DRY in production code and favor DAMP in test code.

Keep Tests Focused

Okay, so we said that readability is king when it comes to test code, but that's not the only thing that keeps them maintainable. Remember the SRP, single responsibility principle? Tests should follow this principle as well, which basically means test one thing at a time. If a test fails, you want to figure out why as quickly as possible, fix it, and move on. What does it mean in practice keeping your tests focused and ensuring they have a single responsibility?

- Verify one thing per test
- 1 assertion per test (some exceptions exist)

- No "if" branching

Well it means you verify one thing per test. If you find yourself saying this test checks this and that, then your test verifies several things, so split it into two, or maybe even three. If you do this, then you should end up with a single assertion per test. Since we are in context of Java, I assume you have written tests before, and you used either JUnit or TestNG. If you haven't, then these assertions look like this.

```java
public class TestExamples {
  @Test
  public void basicMathTest(){
    assertEquals(2, 6/3);
    assertEquals(4, 2*2);
  }
}
```

Here we are asserting basic mathematical operations. And I have a little green arrow over here, and if I run the code, then over here I can see the results. And notice we have two assertions here, one for division and one for multiplication, grouped into one test with defined basicMath operations. And that's bad. Why? Division and multiplication are two separate operations, and they should be tested separately. So if we split the test, we end up with two smaller, but focused tests.

```java
public class TestExamples {
  @Test
  public void divisionWorks(){
    assertEquals(2, 6/3);
  }
  @Test
  public void multiplicationWorks(){
    assertEquals(4, 2*2);
  }
}
```

One verifies just division and has one verification, and the second one verifies multiplication and nothing else. Yes, overall this is more lines of code, but writing tests is not a competition who can write the least amount of code. Finally, watch out for if statements in your tests. If you have them, then it is almost certain that you are testing more than one thing. It's the same with method names if you remember. If your method is named do this and that, then you should split it into two, and if your test has if this or that logic, then again you should split it. Remember, adding if statements adds cyclomatic complexity, and you want to keep that as low as possible in your tests. Ideally your tests should have a calculated cyclomatic complexity of one. So we spoke about writing tests, checking one thing, this has a cost, more lines of code. Do we get any benefits or this? Yes, we do.

Benefit of Focused Tests :
- Fewer points of failure
- Higher stability
- Faster failure investigation
- Overall higher maintainability

First, your tests have fewer points of failure. The concept of point of failure is fairly simple. If you have one assertion, then your test has one reason to fail, excluding obviously environment and other external issues. But if you have five assertions, then your test has five reasons to fail, and that means more unstable tests. So fewer points of failure lead to highly-stable tests. And I promise you, no one likes unstable tests. If they are, they eventually get ignored. Also, if you have just one single reason to fail, instead of five, then you would spend far less time investigating and fixing that test. All of these points lead to the ultimate benefit of overall high test maintainability. Maintainable tests live longer, and their results are actually respected. Constantly-failing tests are ignored because people consider them unreliable, which means all that time spent writing tests becomes wasted.

Use a Test Template

The last practice I would like to highlight is the usage of some kind of template. The vast majority of your tests end up following very similar patterns, and some templates exist to help your team formalize them. One such template is called AAA, which stands for Arrange, Act, Assert. Arrange is the setup, you initialize the objects, you prepare the environment, and you pull some files with test data, for example. Act is where you exercise the functionality you want to test. And finally assert is to verify the output or the resulting behavior.

```
@Test
  public void testOrderExpirationData(){
    // Arrange
    long tomorrow = nowPlusDays(1);
    Order order = new Order();
    // Act
    order.setExpirationDate(tomorrow);
    // Assert
    assertEquals(order.getExpirationDate(),
tomorrow);
  }
```

JUnit and TestNG don't come with such annotations, so I saw teams using comments and basic formatting to visually separate the three stages of each test, and I personally find it quite helpful. A somewhat similar approach is taken by behavior-driven design tests, and they use the keywords Given, When, Then. Given some condition, when we do action A, then we should see the result B. This format has become quite popular because this kind of language closes the gap between technical and nontechnical people. These are some of the most widespread templates or test formats, and quite frankly, none of them is a silver bullet, they're all good, some might be more appropriate in specific scenarios. For example, the AAA is completely fine for unit tests because only developers look at them. And it's also fine for higher-level tests, including browser user interface tests. But if you need to communicate your testing to various nontechnical stakeholders, then adopting the Given, When, Then template might be a better option.

Summary

- Prefer DAMP in tests
- Tests should verify one thing
- Test templates and patterns

This was a fairly brief module, but I hope it was just as useful to you as any other module. We have seen that test code has its own principles and guidelines, and that they are different from production code. DAMP is more important than DRY. As such, readability and how quickly you can understand what the test does is very important. Then, we saw how the SRP can be applied to tests. Each test should focus and verify just one thing. You can have some exceptions to this rule, for example, UI tests in a browser are quite slow, so speed things up, when you load a page, you might want to verify several things at a time, but the cost of that is the introduction of additional points of failure and potential test instability. Finally, we have seen that tests have their own patterns. AAA and BDD style give your tests a convenient and consistent structure.

Module 10 : Maintaining Clean Code

Introduction

This is the last module of this book. We have covered a lot of ground about how to write clean code, but it's never a one-off process. Code keeps evolving, and as such, its quality should also be continuously maintained. In this module, I'm going to try and give you the most practical hands-on tips that are possible to implement almost immediately without long discussions. And to put these tips into some kind of framework, consider this basic two-step programming process. You write code, and then you merge your changes using Git or some other version control system. That's it. And this is fine for your solo home project, but when you are part of a team that builds a large piece of software, these steps are definitely not enough. So let me suggest this longer multistep process that is more likely to keep technical debt at reasonable levels. It will also serve us as an overview of this module. First, you want to agree on at least some basic rules and conventions in your team. Then you write code in line with those conventions. After that, you run a static code analysis tool, that will act as a guide for clean code. Then you submit that code for code review. At the same time, an automatic build would run your unit tests or other tests, and finally you merge after everything is done. This seems like a lot of work, but this is more or less a standard nowadays. And cutting corners at any stage usually means more work later on. So, let's go through this step by step.

Agree on Rules

The first thing that you want to do is agree on some basic rules and conventions, and this is probably the most difficult part. If your team members care about code quality, that's great, but if they don't, you will have to use your selling skills. Just remember one thing, you can't do things alone, you can't be the only one who cares about code quality. Why? Because that's like swimming against the current. You might advance forward a little bit, but without the support and cooperation of others, you will eventually get tired and burn out. Writing clean code is slower than writing bad code because it involves a good deal of thinking. And you alone can't compensate for the rest of the team. So, you all have to be in the same boat, and it might take some time, effort, and discipline for others to get used to it.

Use Static Checkers

Suppose you have written some code or changed existing code, and you are ready to submit your changes. You wrote this code to the best of your ability, so you don't see anything that you would change about it. This is normal, but it doesn't mean that the code is perfect. Regardless if you have a code review process set up, you should use a static analysis tool to check your code. IntelliJ comes with a basic checker, and it highlights the obvious issues.

```java
public class BadCodeSnippets {
    boolean someBoolean; // could be private
    void someOtherMethod(){
        if(someBoolean == true){ // don't compare boolean with true/false
            // ...
        }
        try{
            getFile();
        } catch(IOException ex) {
            ex.printStackTrace();
        }
    }
    private void getFile() throws IOException
    {
```

```
      // get the file
   }
   // Someone else's code
   public int lengthPlus(String str) {
      int len = 2;
      try {
         len += str.length();
      }
      catch (Throwable e) {
         System.out.println("argument was
null");
      }
      return len;
   }
}
```

For example, we have this piece of code highlighted, and if we hover over it, it's telling us that this expression can be simplified. And indeed we have seen that booleans don't need to be compared with true or false, so we can simplify this. This field over here is another example. Again, we hover over it, and it's telling us that the field could be private, so it's suggesting to improve our encapsulation. So we follow the advice and make it private. Such highlighting is not always correct and is not the ultimate authority, but it exists for a reason, so don't ignore it. This in-built code checker is a good start, but is very basic, so I suggest you download and install a third-party plug-in for your IDE. There are multiple, and I will mention just two. The first one is FindBugs, and it has been fairly popular for a number of years, so you might have heard of it. Unfortunately it is not maintained anymore, so this software is functional, but it's slowly dying, so I wouldn't recommend using it. The second tool is called SonarLint. It's open source, and I can highly recommend it. This tool can be installed as a plug-in on the most popular IDEs, IntelliJ, Eclipse, and also Visual Studio, so the same plug-in works for Java, JavaScript, C#, and other languages. Installing it should be a very simple process. In IntelliJ, you would go to General Settings, and under Plugins section, search for sonar, and install it. I already have it installed, I just have it disabled, so I will enable it now and restart IntelliJ.

Boy Scout Rule

Okay, so you did the changes, you ran the static analysis tool, you applied fixes to your own code, but you see that the static analysis tool isn't entirely happy. It's highlighting issues on code that you didn't write and never even touched. What do you do? Fix it or leave it? The answer is it depends. You may have heard of the Boy Scout Rule, leave the campground cleaner than you found it. The very same rule can be applied to code, leave your code better than you found it. And I strongly recommend you use it, but you should be careful. The Boy Scout rule doesn't mean you have to go on an endless refactoring journey. If you finished your task in an hour, and cleaning up some other code would require another hour, then that's probably outside the scope of your task. Here's a quick and simple flowchart to help you make the decision.

Let's say you found some code that needs improvement, ask yourself, do I have to change it to complete my task? Yes, do it. If it's unrelated, then ask yourself another question, is this a small and simple change? You should decide for yourself what that means. I generally consider changes small if they take no more than 10, 20 minutes of additional time, but it can be more or less. So, if it's small, then re-factor it. If it's not that small, then either leave it as is or, and that's always better, add a TODO comment with an issue ticket if you have an issue tracking system. We discussed comments and TODOs in another module. A single small change isn't going to bring noticeable benefit. However, a thousand small changes done over a year will definitely have an impact. I've seen an entire code base transformed from spaghetti to something actually pleasant to work with when this rule was applied for a long enough period of time. Try it out, be patient, and see for yourself.

Code Review and Pair Programming

So, you are finally ready to submit your changes. And here we have two potential scenarios. Your team either has a code review process in place or it doesn't. If it does, then here are some tips for more effective code reviewing.

Good Code Review :

- At least two reviewers
- At least one person understands the business side of the code under review
- Merging not possible until all highlighted issues addressed

At least two people should look at your code. That's the standard I have seen throughout several jobs. However, I understand that teams can be small or everyone is under pressure to finish their own task. So if that's the case, one reviewer is fine as well. After all, a second pair of eyes is better than none. Also, ideally one person reviewing your code should understand the business side and the background of the task you're trying to complete. Of course code review stage is not business analysis stage, but I have seen a situation where a team member submitted good, clean code, but because he misunderstood the requirements, the code didn't do what it was supposed to do. Something like if a client wanted a 4x4 car and instead got a racing car, the racing car is great, but that's not what was supposed to be done. Finally, merging of the changes should be possible only if both reviewers explicitly approve them, and all highlighted issues were addressed, meaning if your code received two comments, you should respond to those comments, for example, yes, I have fixed as per your suggestion, or no, that's not how it works because reason X and reason Y. Needless to say, code review should be done through a tool that also has an automatic build job that runs your tests, but that's more of a devops topic. To all of this you might say, well, we don't have any code review tool set up. In that case, I can only recommend that someone sets it up; however, that's not something that can be achieved in a single day. So as an immediate solution, I can suggest you practice pair programming, or at least carry out the code review by looking at each other's screens. No tool needed, just say hey, could you please come over here and spend 5 minutes, scan through my code, and tell me if you see any obvious mistakes. It might seem unusual at first, but I have seen this work, especially in smaller teams. Eternal vigilance is the price of all quality, and adapting to new habits will help you achieve it.

Summary

Time to wrap up our module and the entire book.
- Use static code analysis tools
- Apply the Boy scout rule
- Code Review and Pair Programming

In this module, we have seen that writing code is by far not the only thing we can and should do. We should use static code analysis tools that will quickly and reliably find a large number of issues that we wouldn't otherwise notice. Preventing problems is always better and cheaper than fixing them later. And tools such as SonarLint will help you achieve just that. We then talked about the Boy Scout rule. You should develop a positive attitude to making small improvements here and there. A lot of people normally say this code isn't mine, or this code was already there when I opened the file, but that's not great. Instead, we should train ourselves to think hey, I could spend just a couple of extra minutes and make this code better. Finally, we have seen how code review is another way of preventing bugs and issues. If you don't have something in place, try and set it up. If not, start small, and review each other's code by doing some pair programming. This concludes our module and book.

www.ingramcontent.com/pod-product-compliance
Lightning Source LLC
Chambersburg PA
CBHW070841070326
40690CB00009B/1646